FILIPINO CHILDREN
UNDER STRESS

Feb. 10, '90

Dear Jammy!

May this book help us be
better parents to the boys.

Love,

MARIA LOURDES ARELLANO-CARANDANG

FILIPINO CHILDREN UNDER STRESS
Family Dynamics and Therapy

ATENEO DE MANILA UNIVERSITY PRESS
QUEZON CITY, METRO MANILA 1987

ATENEO DE MANILA UNIVERSITY PRESS
Loyola Heights, Quezon City
P.O. Box 154, Manila

Copyright 1987 by Ateneo de Manila
ISBN 971-113-065-3
Second Printing 1988

Illustration for cover by
Christopher Franz Carandang, seven years old

To the cherished memory of

MAMA, PAPA, and CITAS

And to my own living family—

my husband TITO, my children

RICKY, RAFA, and CHRIS

Foreword

SHE HAS ALWAYS BEEN CALLED "HONEY" by her friends and cop-sychologists as if to indicate how much loved she is. Children, too, take to her as the proverbial fly to honey. This mutual attraction to children, together with her Ph.D. in Clinical Psychology from the University of California at Davis, has made Maria Lourdes Arellano-Carandang the foremost child psychologist in the Philippines today.

And now, she has summed up more than a decade of clinical experience in a marvelous book that is as alive as the children in her play therapy room. She unfolds her approach to children in distress. The child is not the abnormal one. Rather, it is the family that is suffering stress. The child, the vulnerable one, by his behavior is merely reporting the family's distress. Thus healing must focus on the family as a whole system. The family is the patient rather than the individual.

The whole Filipino family enters into the problem and has a part in its therapy: parents, children, *ate*, *kuya*, *lolo*, *lola*; even the *yaya*. Each has a part to play because the family is so close that "any stress or pain experienced by one member is felt and reacted to in some way by all the members of the family, each in his or her own way." Likewise, the family has individual resources that can be harnessed in the therapeutic process.

Case histories out of real Philippine life give a succession of insights into the workings of Filipino family life. There is the maiden aunt or the *lola* who may hold the strings of power and who has to be won over before therapy can proceed. There is the child given over to the grandparents to provide them company and in turn to receive an education. There is the child who takes on the function of *tagasaló*, taking responsibility for duties left unfulfilled by the parents. The book is an insight-giving mirror into our own lives. It should be read not only by psychologists but also by all parents who wish to understand their own families better.

The book makes for easy reading and is painless as an instruction manual. The concepts simultaneously come out from the case examples. Merely reading the book gives one an understanding of family therapy, its theory and practice.

— JAIME C. BULATAO, S.J.

Preface

THIS BOOK COMES OUT OF A NEED to share my experience and insights as a clinical psychologist and, more specifically, as a child and family therapist helping Filipino families cope with stress. In response to this, I have been slowly evolving, for more than a decade now, a modified and workable child and family therapy approach which can be used in the treatment of Filipino families who come for psychological help.

Much has been said about the close family ties in the Filipino family. Our families have generally been described as closely knit and cohesive—the solid and basic foundation of Filipino society. Unfortunately, however, the solidarity of the Filipino family in the past decade has been seriously threatened by marked economic, sociopolitical, and moral crises in the country. The crises have intensified in the past five years and finally culminated in February 1986, when People Power overthrew the dictatorship.

The existing intrafamilial stresses have been further strained by these extrafamilial societal stresses. The stresses experienced in daily living with family members, such as marital conflicts, sibling rivalry, favoritism, finding one's place in the family, and the like (Carandang 1979) were enough to make families seek psychological help. But the difficult times brought about by Marcos's autocratic rule, coupled with the recent drastic changes in the sociopolitical order in the country, have created an even more tremendous impact on family cohesiveness. As the burden carrier of the social order, the family has become a bottleneck, absorbing a lot of these stresses. Perhaps, it has absorbed more than it has been able to cope with in the past. The breakdown and disintegration of the Filipino family has become a real concern among psychologists, sociologists and economists; but nowhere is the crisis more truly felt than among family members themselves, namely, the parents, grandparents, and the children.

Although this observation is undoubtedly shared by both professionals and family members alike, not much has been written as to how families actually cope with stress and better yet, how they can be helped to cope with stress more effectively. One can posit several questions in relation to this, such as: How do families perceive these stresses as they experience them? How do they make sense of these strains and conflicts? What is the collective impact of these stresses on the family system as a whole?

With these questions in mind, there is definitely a need to look deeper into the family system. There is a need to understand the Filipino family more intimately, to dig into the "guts" of the culture, and to get into the inner dynamics of the family members as they live together through these stresses. The clinical approach enables us to penetrate deeply into the inner world of the family and to capture its members' experiences at the deepest level. This being an indigenous approach, it allows us, in a sense, to get a glimpse of the culture's soul (Carandang 1985).

Using the clinical approach, I have written this book primarily for the use of therapists — psychologists, psychiatrists, social workers, psychiatric nurses, and guidance counselors — who work with children and their families. To protect the identity of persons involved, I have changed the names and certain details in the cases presented.

I have exerted a lot of effort toward a straigthforward presentation of cases, writing in simple language the underlying dynamics, theory, and intervention strategies. My special concern is for this book to be comprehensible to parents and teachers, for them to gain from these concepts a good grasp, a greater understanding of children with special problems. Those who want additional technical material can look up the references cited from the literature; a sample evaluation form is also provided in the appendix. A discussion of concepts and specific technical terms used in the text can be found in each chapter to maximize learning.

The book is organized along the following lines.

Chapter 1 gives an overview of basic concepts in family systems theory in an unorthodox manner. Concepts are not defined per se; rather their meanings can be "painlessly absorbed" in a semiexperiential learning process from the actual case examples. Bandler (1985) might call this as learning with the right-brain versus the usual left-brain approach. This approach is used throughout the book.

Chapter 2 situates some common family stresses within the country's sociopolitical context and presents the results of a miniresearch study on poor urban families alongside results of studies on families from a higher socioeconomic class.

Chapter 3 presents cases on broken families where children have to cope with marital discord and separation. Some intervention strategies are also suggested.

Chapter 4, "The Family Caretaker," dramatically portrays how a young child tries to take care of his troubled family, and how this initially appears to be childhood suicide.

Chapter 5, "The Tagasalo or Mananalo Syndrome," tackles at length the compulsive taking-care syndrome in adults, especially among Filipino women.

Chapter 6 poses the important question often asked: How does a family cope with a special child? This chapter also discusses family dynamics in raising special children — one autistic, one retarded, one gifted, and another, an adopted child.

Chapter 7 reverses the question posed in chapter 6: How does a not-so-special child find his place in a special, or exceptional, family?

Chapter 8 looks into the delicate topic of suicide in the family and goes deeper into the dynamics involved through an in-depth presentation of one case. It involves suicide-by-hanging in two generations of a large extended family.

Chapter 9 tackles a very interesting and useful question in family therapy: "Who has the power in the family?" Some emerging patterns are presented—the sick *lola* (grandmother), the *tiya* (financier aunt), and the all-knowing *yaya* (child caretaker).

The Postscript tries to integrate briefly the basic insights gathered from the cases presented, with family systems theory and therapy as the running thread.

I have chosen those topics and cases that stood out in my own experiential map. I have found them substantial enough to learn from. It is my hope that the reader will learn from them as well.

I would like to express my sincere thanks to the families who have shared their inner lives with me. I hope they will feel rewarded by the help they will now bring to others through this book.

Through its faculty research grants, the Ateneo de Manila University gave me financial assistance for the study that went into this book. I acknowledge this help with gratitude.

Contents

1

Basic Concepts of Family Therapy

THIS CHAPTER WILL ILLUSTRATE some basic concepts of the family systems approach in the context of the Filipino family. The first seven cases on children's reaction to stress form the main part of this chapter. At the end of the chapter, there is a brief review of the literature and a discussion of the concepts used. Concepts therefore are not defined in the traditional manner. Rather, their meanings emerge from the dynamics of the cases presented. In this way, readers may find themselves understanding the concepts as they are formally introduced in a process similar to experiential learning. The subsequent chapters will use this same approach.

The Child and the Family in Stress

More often than not, the stresses experienced in the family are absorbed and acted out by its most vulnerable members — the children. I cite the following case in point. Mario, a seven year-old boy, started to indulge in petty stealing and lying. The political crisis brought about by the Aquino assassination caused sudden financial setbacks in his family. Mario's father had lost his job, and Mario and his sisters were told that they might not be able to go back to school, where they were doing very well. Mario was the middle sibling and the only boy in the family. His elder sister was nine years old, while his younger sister was four. As the tension mounted, fighting among the siblings intensified, and the parents were at a loss as to how to deal with the stress. They found themselves scolding Mario frequently, at the same time complaining about him: "We are already having so many problems and, instead of helping, he is adding to the burden! Now he is our big problem."

During the initial therapy session, Mario had obviously become the only focus of his family's attention. Steps were taken so that he would not be immediately branded as a "bad boy," or the family scapegoat. In the session, everyone in the family realized and clearly verbalized for the first time that all of them were under tremendous stress and strain. Mario was merely acting out the "uncontainable" tension for them. Mario's "stealing" behavior was not the problem. It was merely the result of his family's disequilibrium; his behavior was his way of trying to help them solve their problem.

In his own ineffective way, Mario was actually trying to do something about the problem. Mario had become the IP, the Identified Patient, or the DP, the Designated Patient (Bowen 1978,Minuchin 1967 and Andolfi 1979). French (1979)would call him the "symptom carrier" of a family in a state of crisis or disequilibrium.

In the therapy sessions, it was important to enable members of Mario's family to view his behavior in the afore-mentioned perspective. They had first to recognize and accept that they were all under stress, and then ask themselves how they were individually dealing with the stress. Each member was experiencing the crisis, and each was coping with, or surviving it in his or her own way. Most of the time, families deny a problem of this kind, and family members are careful not to talk about it in the hope that the problem will go away by itself.

Mario's behavior was seen as a signal of a cry for help, calling attention to his family's problem. It was the most obvious reaction to the stress. This eventually paved the way for the realization that if they worked together, Mario and his family could assess the situation and have some control over it.

It very often happens that when a family is undergoing a crisis, its members unknowingly turn against one another to relieve their frustration and anger about it. If they do not stop and recognize that they are all under severe stress, they may fail to understand that essentialy their common enemy is actually the stressful event, not one another.

In the case of Mario, his family started working as a team after grasping his "problem" from a family perspective and deciding the whole family had to solve the "problem."

To augment their family income, the children began selling stickers. The mother's source of income, earlier taken for granted, was now appreciated and given importance. As they discussed the problem as a family, they spent more time together, developed closer relationships, and thereby stopped blaming one another's behavior for the problem (Satir 1967).

More importantly, as a family, they experienced a sense of power and competence in dealing with stress by pulling their resources together, instead of taking things out on one another.

Another case involved Alma, a ten-year-old girl, who was normally quiet. A few weeks before her family sought professional help, however, she started screaming and acting aggressively toward everybody in the family. Once, at the height of her anger, she pushed her cousin into the swimming pool, causing the cousin to almost drown. These "sudden" outbursts shocked and alarmed her parents and her older brother, thereby prompting them to bring Alma for therapy. Why had she changed so suddenly?

As it turned out, the family had just moved from a spacious house to a smaller one, because they could no longer afford the rent on the bigger house. In a span of six months, the maid who had served them for thirteen years left them; the family's pet chimpanzee died; Alma's mother got pregnant — her third since she gave birth ten years ago (it was a difficult pregnancy, too), and Alma even saw a cat giving birth. The family was definitely in a crisis, but no one was openly recognizing, discussing, and sharing the stress. The family was simply overwhelmed by it. They were ignoring the tension, as though such a response would make it disappear magically. In the meantime, everyone was feeling drained, short-tempered, and irritable. The child's behavior, again, in this case, can be seen as a red flag — a cry for help. She was saying, "Help, my family is drowning!"

The parents could not accept and recognize the overwhelming stress that the family was experiencing. Instead, they tried to deny the intense feelings accompanying this crisis and tried to "sweep them under the rug." This leads us to one principle in family systems approach which states that the family cannot *sweep tension under the rug for a long time:* "Something's gotta give somewhere" (French 1977).

A third case involved Danilo, an eight-year-old who refused to go to school after his father left for Saudi Arabia to earn more so that his struggling family could make both ends meet. He was beset by all kinds of fears. The mother became very distraught because Danilo had always been an honor student. He started to clam up and became very inhibited to a point that his body became rigid and stiff, as if to contain and protect his inner feelings. The mother, on the other hand, was a very nervous woman who was dependent on her husband. She had an extremely difficult time adjusting to her husband's absence but she denied her fears and loneliness, and instead focused on Danilo's problematic behavior. During the therapy session, Danilo's mother was able to accept that she herself felt lonely and helpless and this feeling made it impossible for her to help Danilo. She realized she was clinging to Danilo who, in turn, was just trying to "take care" of his mother. Danilo had to be with his mother at all times, so that nothing would happen to her. At the same time, he had a strong fear of losing another parent. As the sessions progressed, the mother was helped to regain her sense of adequacy and competence (e.g., she was a good cook, an efficient housekeeper, a loving mother) — something that she thought she had lost.

As she regained her equilibrium, her unrecognized strengths and creative talents resurfaced and they were used to help Danilo cope with his own fears. Such awareness essentially changed the family system since the two elements, i.e., the mother's own adequacy and her sense of competence, paved the way for Danilo's conquest of his inhibition. Danilo now felt more "free" and did not have to try so hard to take care of his mother. (How the child acts as the caretaker of the family will be discussed further in chapter 4.) It is also important to state that, in the process, the mother was initially helped by her *ate* (elder sister) who was guided by the therapist. This manner of making use of resources in the extended family is usually helpful when it is done with the awareness that dependency is not merely to be transferred to another person. Care must be taken because — without proper guidance and awareness — dependency may, more often than not, be further encouraged in the process. After too long a period of time, the person who is being depended upon may feel the burden too heavy to carry. In this case, the mother and her *ate* were guided so that the former's dependency was not merely transferred to her *ate*. She instead learned to trust her own abilities.

Another reaction to stress was shown by Toto, a four-year-old boy who became encopretic; he began soiling his pants, despite being toilet-trained since he was two years of age. His father was a political detainee, and Toto was disturbed because he could not comprehend why his father had been jailed. He would incessantly ask his mother, "Is Papa a bad guy? Why is he in jail?" His mother, however, did not know how to explain his father's detention to him; she was herself struggling to contain her own angry feelings toward the then unjust and dictatorial political system that was too powerful for her to confront.

As a result, the mother underwent individual therapy and gained the support from a member of the family — in this case the maternal grandmother. Toto likewise underwent therapy but of a different nature. He joined play therapy with a group of children who were in a similar predicament. From this group he drew psychological support and assurance. During the play therapy sessions, he was able to release and express his pent-up anger and he realized he was not alone in that situation. The children improvised games, such as "Punish the bad soldiers," or fantasized about a superhero rescuing the detainees or a child outsmarting the guards. In this way, through projective fantasy play in a group format, they experienced their own sense of power over the oppressive situation.

There was also the case of Nena, a nine-year-old girl whose bed-wetting became frequent whenever the marital conflict between her parents would intensify. This prompted me to call her the "family barometer" (Carandang 1979). In this case, marital therapy was the initial step taken, and it was used as the entry point into the family system.

There was also a time when I was seeing a seven-year-old named Carlo along with his mother, who was a single parent, for conjoint therapy. She was a public schoolteacher who lived with her mother. Carlo started to act out his frustrations by hurting others and telling lies. His mother had exhausted all disciplinary measures — from patient explanations to severe punishments — but Carlo continued to act as if he never heard anything she had said. After a few sessions, there did not seem to be any progress. In other words, the therapy was not moving — some "sabotage" was going on somewhere, so to speak. It turned out that in this small family, the *lola* called the shots, overruled all the mother's moves, even those involving disciplinary measures. It became clear therefore that the *lola* was the real power in the family. Knowing the real power in the family is very important in deciding the most effective strategy to be undertaken (French 1977). However, discerning where power lies can get to be complicated at times. It may lie in the hands of a sick mother or a rich, unmarried aunt who is living with the family and who has the all-important financial resources. In the case of Carlo, I asked his *lola* to join the therapy session, when I discovered it was she who wielded the power. Not surprisingly, it was only thereafter that changes began to take place.

A graphic illustration of the issue of power was seen in the case of Mark, a bright and sensitive five-year-old who first arrived at my clinic accompanied by his mother, grandmother, and great-grandmother — a scenario involving four generations. Mark was clearly at the bottom of the totem pole with three generations of domineering females above him! It was no wonder then that Mark was observed to be overcautious, fearful, and terribly passive. In this case, therapy necessitated the inclusion of all three maternal generations. (More discussion on power will be presented in chapter 9, since the aim of this chapter is to introduce basic concepts, and not to explain the cases in great detail. These and other concepts will be encountered again in the next chapters.)

There are many cases which illustrate that the dynamics of the Filipino family system are not so easily deciphered.

One has to look into the total living unit or **the Filipino "family"** (Laing 1969) in order to know what the family system actually consists of. It may include the grandparents, an unmarried aunt who is supporting the whole family financially, an uncle, the *yaya* who knows the child more intimately, a cousin whose parents live in the province, or an unmarried daughter with several children. In our extended family system, the child can get lost and may have a difficult time finding a way to be recognized as a unique person. To satisfy his needs, he has to attune himself to the different adults in the family, as well as to his siblings. Aside from this, he may have to contend with the presence of his aunts, uncles, the *ate* or the *kuya* (older brother). In such an interwoven system, the dynamics and inter-relationships become more intricate, and a lot of *pakiramdaman* (feeling out) is involved. The child, feeling overwhelmed by these conditions, may consequently learn not to verbalize his or her feelings directly and simply, most especially if these are negative feelings toward the adults in the family. He may thus unconsciously express himself through "misbehavior" (Carandang 1979).

"In a systemic approach," Andolfi (1979) says, "human beings and events are studied in terms of their interactions rather than their intrinsic characteristics." **Symptomatic behavior** is a signal of the rigid structuring of family relationships. It protects an equilibrium that has been constructed around a conflictual situation which eventually becomes functional. Instead of classifying an individual's behavior, we try to decipher the meaning of this behavior with respect to the family context in which it occurs.

It is therefore a basic concept in family systems theory that **any stress or pain experienced by one member is felt and reacted to in some way by all the members of the family, each in his or her own way** (French 1977, Andolfi 1979, Satir 1967, Bowen 1978, and Minuchin 1967).

Therapy therefore can initially include all or some selected members of the household, even as the therapist assesses that there is a need for them to be involved in the therapeutic process. In therapy, the most important consideration is the harnessing of all existing resources within the household and family as the therapist helps them to support themselves.

Further Discussion

Until the 1950s, family therapy was an underground movement: The theories it espoused where either unheard of, unrecognized, or ignored. It was psychoanalysis that showed its power and control, and therapists strictly adhered to the principles of safeguarding personal privacy and the sacredness of the one-to-one therapist-patient relationship (Bowen 1976).

As the field of therapy became less "traditional," however, and other methods besides psychoanalysis were practised, therapists introduced more creative and innovative therapy techniques. They became aware of interactions and interrelationships in behavior among people, which more than ever called for resourcefulness and creativity in the practice of the therapeutic art.

In the Philippines, family therapy has been a controversial issue since 1980. At present, only a few practise it, and very selectively at that, because getting family members together for therapy sessions is very difficult.

In a recent convention among psychiatrists, some senior psychiatrist-professors were asked if family therapy would be a workable approach for Filipinos. The answers were negative. One reason cited was that Filipinos do not usually communicate directly with one another and seeing the whole family together in therapy would therefore be useless and not suited to the culture. But should not this very reason cited against family therapy be utilized to argue for its usefulness? The fact that we need to communicate more clearly with each other to resolve existing family conflicts all the more calls for its use. Indeed, as more trained family therapists have begun to practise, the need for family therapy has become more evident.

The methods and techniques used in Filipino family therapy, however, differ from those of the West, since the composition of our families and our ways of relating with one another differ from those of the West. Although techniques — such as the use of the *ate* or *kuya*, the *lola*, or the inclusion of the yaya, and the like — are similar to some Western methods, the more subtle ways of making family members confront issues are uniquely Filipino. Still, the basic theory remains the same. As I have stated earlier, the stresses in a family are always felt interactively, such that the stress undergone or the pain felt by one member affects all the other family members in some way.

There is one difficulty, though, that traditionally trained therapists face in doing family therapy: The **shift in perspective.** Earlier, the focus was the individual as the patient; today the **family is the patient.**

To aid students of family therapy in making this shift, one very effective way is for them to think of a metaphor that will capture the essence of the family, starting from their own families (Laing 1969). I find it even helps further when they are made to visualize and draw or diagram this metaphor. For example, one graduate student pictured her family as a hanging mobile, since everyone in her family seemed just to be coming and going all the time: "While some are studying or working out of town or outside the country, others would be arriving from the province, and so on," she captioned her drawing.

Another student thought of her family as a flock of sheep with her mother as the shepherd and she, the last lamb in the line. She was the youngest in a family of ten — all achievers — and she was constantly feeling intimidated and overwhelmed. Her mother is a successful physician.

Another student could not think of a metaphor for his family, because they had not really been staying together for sometime. He could not think of something that would capture the **Gestalt**. After a while, he had an insight — and the word and the image of a "shipwreck" came to him.

Figure 1 shows a family at the crossroads, with everyone rushing off to work or school and barely having time to talk with one another. It clearly captures the hurried and harassed pace of a family system where, if you stand still at a fixed point, you will be left behind and, consequently, left out. Figure 2 uses the metaphor of a stream. The student likens her family to a "flowing stream," with the rocks or big stones as problems that hinder the smooth flow.

Students have reported how "liberating" it is for them to find the metaphor for their family. It gives them a certain amount of distancing and a perspective that is helpful for themselves, as well as for their families. They are momentarily able to come out of their feeling of being totally immersed or buried in a tense situation, and thus they gain a more total and objective view of their family system and its problems. This is also therapeutic in itself and can become a valuable part in the healing process.

Another distinct and beneficial effect of this metaphorical perspective is that it enables the family therapist to view the system as a whole entity, thereby putting himself or herself "on top of the situation." After all, the family therapist has to be in command of the entire process.

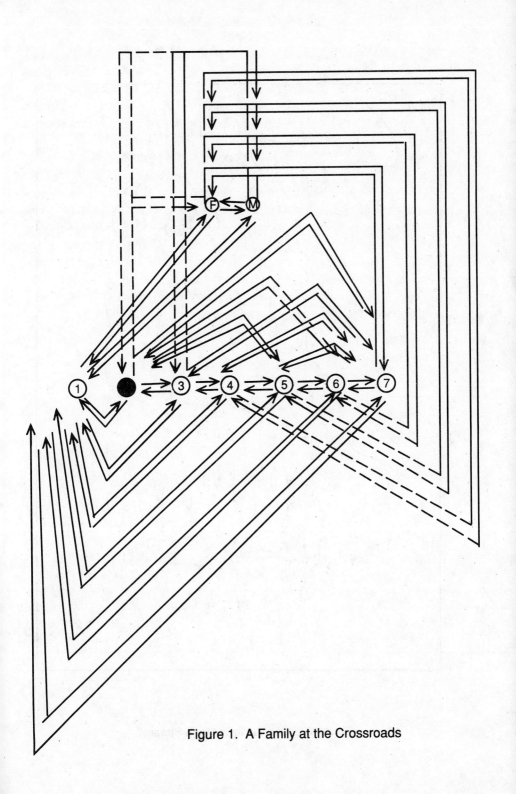

Figure 1. A Family at the Crossroads

Figure 2.   "Our Family Is Like a Stream."

2

Common Family Stresses in the Sociopolitical Context

I INTRODUCED SOME KEY CONCEPTS of family therapy in chapter 1 by citing varied case examples from my own clinical practice. Since these basic concepts of the family systems approach have been illustrated, we can now apply them to more specific examples that are similar in at least one respect. These are the case studies of troubled families whose stresses and problems are the direct effects of the sociopolitical crises that rocked the Philippines in the wake of the Aquino assassination and the events leading to the February 1986 Revolution. In order to further situate the stresses experienced by these families in the context of the larger society, I will discuss in detail my investigative research into poor urban families. These family experiences will be analyzed in the light of family systems dynamics against the background of sociopolitical confrontations.

Before going into the study on poor urban families, I shall refer to an earlier paper which depicts three families from the upper middle-income group (Carandang 1984). Although the study in the paper did not use the method of the study on poor urban families, it provides useful data on families from a different socioeconomic class.

The Family as Source of Conflict

Even before the onset of martial law in 1972, the lower socioeconomic class, which constitutes the greatest segment of the Philippine population, had to contend with the hardships of daily life. The children of the poor had to help their families earn a living, oftentimes to the detriment of their education, ironically the only probable means to alleviate their poverty.

Consistent with their meager financial resources and limited opportunities, these children oftentimes find themselves working as sidewalk vendors, itinerant cigarette and sampaguita vendors, watch-your-car boys and girls, or sellers of plastic bags.

Marcos's autocractic rule failed to improve the quality of life of the average citizen. Its entrenchment even worsened the moral degradation which seeped into contemporary Filipino life. A concrete example is the active propagation of tourism through the highly publicized "come-on" of child prostitution, a phenomenon hitherto unknown in the Philippines. Another well-known phenomenon is the exodus of migrant workers to the Middle East, which has caused the separation of parents from children in many Filipino families. There was also cynicism among the youth, owing to their lack of faith in the leaders of our country. This crisis in leadership definitely affected the attitudes of the young people deeply.

Placed in the context of these societal stresses, the family is often perceived to be a reliable source of support in times of difficulties. At the same time, though, it can also be the source of conflicts.

We have seen how the modern family lives in a state of tension because it is the "burden carrier of the social order" (Bowen 1978, French 1977, and Minuchin 1967). In a society where rapid and confusing social and political changes are taking place, the problems outnumber the solutions. The resulting uncertainties are absorbed by members of society who are in turn members of families.

Being the unit eyed as the possible source of problems, the family is the social structure par excellence that intimately reflects the stresses and strains of social life. Thus, a healthy family today is not only the focal point of frustrations and tensions but also the source of strategies for resolving these frustrations and for easing these tensions.

As we have discussed in the previous chapter, the family systems theorists state that stresses in the family are always experienced interactively; that is, the stress undergone or the pain felt by one member inevitably affects all the other members in some way (Andolfi 1979). Oftentimes, the reaction is more evidently exhibited by the more vulnerable members of the family — the children.

At this point, let me review three cases that illustrate how some family stresses have been brought about by the sociopolitical crises arising from the morally degrading effects of martial law. These were three in-depth cases of the crises of the times (Carandang 1984). The experiences came about at the height of graft and corruption in the government; and both rich and poor had to deal with the economic, social, and moral hardships of the times. These case studies were aimed at obtaining a greater understanding of the dynamics of stresses, and coping among Filipino families as viewed from the societal context so described. These are in line with the view shared by Minuchin (1974), that therapists should look at families in the context of the community. To carry out the investigation, intrafamilial as well as extrafamilial stresses — and the interaction of these — were analyzed. Moreover, the family systems approach, as opposed to the individual approach, was chosen so as to obtain a better perspective of the dynamics going on within the family. Analysis of the data also revealed the coping mechanisms of families as they reacted to the impact of sociopolitical crises. In the process of interpreting the different observations, an integrated view of the families' stress-handling strategies is also explicitly discussed.

These three cases of urban middle-to-higher income families revealed that one or both parents were directly involved in such political activities as rallies and demonstrations, manifesting the growing opposition to the Marcos government.

In all three cases, the stress was very strongly felt in an already-strained marital relationship. While the wife was trying to make do with a static budget, the economic situation caused further strain, and the husband had to work for longer hours. This left the husband with little time for the wife and children. The wife expressed feelings of rejection and complained that the husband cared more for his buddies in the office than for his family. She felt that the office was first and the family was only second in the husband's list of priorities.

The wife—whose husband was involved in political activities—felt that the loyalty of her husband was to political action and no longer to the family. While the husband would insist it was necessary to give his time and effort to the country during those critical times, the wife felt the family must be his first priority.

In the case of a couple where the wife was the one involved in political action, it was the husband who felt the family must come first in her order of priorities.

The third case involved a preadolescent boy, Martin. The strain expressed itself in a generalized attitude of extreme hostility. Martin became so hostile that his classmates could no longer tolerate him. They ostracized him and ganged up on him; at one time, they even used his face to erase the blackboard. It then became necessary for his parents to let him drop out of school.

In this particular case, there was overt hostility in Martin's house. This took the form of constant arguments between his parents. It turned out that they had different approaches to current political problems. The mother got so involved in rallies such that she would be often absent from the house, while the father was secretly collecting ammunition for a more drastic action against government authorities. An important intrafamilial factor to consider was the father's long-standing and deeply rooted hostility against his own father — Martin's grandfather. This intense hostility was triggered and aggravated by the dictatorial leadership in the country at the time.

As the stresses in these marriages became increasingly burdensome, the children in these families reacted in their own unique ways. In one, the seven-year-old child indulged in petty stealing, when previously, he was well-behaved. It was as if he signalled and mirrored out the stress in the family.

Another case involved a five-year-old boy who tried to get a ten-peso bill from the therapist's handbag. When pressed for an explanation, he said he wanted to have some money for his father's birthday. He wanted to buy his father a gift to make him happy. At another time, the same boy expressed a desire to die. This alarmed his parents. Further probing, however, revealed that he wanted to die so that he could go to heaven and be with God. Being in heaven, he believed he could be strong and powerful. He would thus be able to help his family on earth.

In the case of Dondi, a sixteen-year-old adolescent, the stress was felt in an overall feeling of disillusionment and cynicism. He sadly stated that, with the unfortunate state of society, there was no one he could believe in any more. Though he talked about his and his classmates' increasing disenchantment, the optimism and idealism of youth came through when he declared that, someday, he would like to enter politics "to correct all these injustices."

These data provide an "inner view" of the stresses experienced by middle-to-high income families as they adjust to the economic, social and political crises of the period (Carandang 1984).

Of similar importance is the picture of how poor urban families perceived the stresses in the context of the sociopolitical crises. More revealing are the coping mechanisms used by such families.

The data come from a small and poor urban community of 215 families in Quezon City. Parents of the families were skilled or semiskilled workers — carpenters, construction workers, drivers, roof repairmen (*latero*), beauticians, mailmen, sidewalk vendors, women who ironed clothes for a living (*tagaplantsa*), and the like. The largest family had fifteen children, while the smallest had only two. Six was the average number of children in the families. Parents earned an average of thirty pesos daily. Their educational attainment varied — some had no education at all, while others were elementary and high school graduates. Their average length of stay in the community ranged from three to forty-eight years.

Methods used in this study were similar to participant observation. The assistant researcher worked with these families for four years prior to the actual research. All the while, she made weekly visits of at least three to four hours each visit. This made it possible for twenty families to be interviewed in-depth at least three times.

Familiarity and rapport were clearly evident as the assistant researcher and I entered the community. The children called us *ate* and invited both of us to come into their homes. Mothers and fathers who were at home during the interviews seemed to welcome the opportunity to talk about their problems. It came to a point where both men and women voiced out their grievances so much so that some cried during the interviews.

In the community, a typical working day would find the wife working at home, housecleaning, washing clothes, and drawing water from the well — accompanied by her children, usually the girls. Occasionally, though, the boys would also help in getting water. Meanwhile, the men would be out working to earn some money, although some were unemployed and merely stayed home. During weekdays, they would sit together chatting, playing board games or reading *komiks* and magazines. During weekends, the men would gather together and drink liquor at the neighborhood store.

On the other hand, the children would be playing, helping with the household chores, taking care of younger siblings, or preparing for school.

Most of the time, the eldest female child, or *ate*, busied herself with the household chores. She was responsible for taking care of her younger siblings, and they would run to her whenever they were caught in a fight or needed help in their schoolwork.

Amid all their economic problems, a number of families still managed to celebrate nuptials or the baptism of a child by having a feast, or *handa*, even if they had to borrow money for the occasion.

For the purpose of making hypotheses about family dynamics, as well as to obtain different viewpoints, three people were interviewed in each of the twenty families under study, namely, the husband, the wife, and a child. The child-interviewee was usually the one most willing and able to communicate among the children. The children interviewed had ages ranging from seven to twenty-one years.

Respondents were asked whom they considered the "stressors," i.e., those that caused great stress in the family. The respondents ranked their respective stressors from the most to the least stress-causing. These stressors were ranked and weighted, with the first stressor being the one who caused the greatest amount of stress. The results of the survey are tabulated below:

Rank Stressors

A. Wives

1.0	*asawa* (husband)
2.5	*pera* (money)
2.5	*kapitbahay at kamag-anak* (neighbors and relatives)
4.0	*anak* (child)

B. Husbands

1.0	*pera* (money)
2.0	*komunidad* (community)
3.0	*anak* (child)
4.0	*asawa* (wife)

C. Children

1.0	*pansin* (attention)
2.0	pag-aaral (education)
	magulang (parents)

While the wives ranked *asawa* (husband) as the most frequent stressor among the four mentioned, the husbands ranked wives only as the fourth, or the least of four stressors, the first being *pera* (money). When asked further to explain their choice, the wives cited *pangangaliwa* (infidelity), *nambubugbog* (physical abuse, or wife-beating), *walang trabaho* (unemployed) and *lasenggo* (drunkard) as reasons. They expressed their frustration and helplessness over these. While they dutifully performed their roles as mothers and housekeepers — and, for some, even as wage-earners — they said they felt neglected by their husbands. In this regard, one could only speculate that their husbands were either not aware of this neglect, or were ignorant that they were the source of marital problems, or did not consider their responsibility of major concern to their wives.

In terms of marital relationship dynamics, it can be hypothesized that the husbands and wives did not see eye to eye. While the wife needed attention and loyalty from her husband as she conscientiously performed her duties, the husband was more interested in activities outside of the family's scope, such as looking for jobs or for diversions in the form of extramarital relationships. In this way, the husband's mind would perhaps be temporarily freed from being preoccupied with his inability to fulfill his roles as husband and provider. This finding is similar to what is cited in a study by Jurilla (1986) on rural couples.

Insofar as finances were concerned, a husband stated that, in spite of working for twelve hours a day, his earnings were not enough to sustain the needs of his family. Problems regarding money were never thought to be tied up with the unjust condition within the larger social system. As a concrete microview of this particular community, money problems were experienced probably in relation to the husband's unemployment. The family could thus only live in a community where the families are of meager means like them. It did not occur to them that their needy plight could be due to the unequal distribution of resources in the society where they live. In other words, the stresses of survival did not perhaps allow them to analyze their difficult condition on a macroscopic level vis-à-vis the society as a whole.

Next to financial concerns, husband and wife experience stress from factors stemming within the community. The husbands generalized these as simply *komunidad*, while the wives were more concrete and specific by identifying *kapitbahay* and *kamag-anak* to be the sources of their stress and conflict. More specifically, they referred to *tsismis* (gossip), *intriga* (intrigues), and *nagagalit sa anak ng iba* (scolding children other than their own). These irritations would be compounded by the husband who, being more concerned with leadership in the community, would advise the wife to simply ignore these neighborhood goings-on. In her intimate day-to-day relationships with neighbors, however, the wife often found it impossible to do so.

Notwithstanding the above-mentioned factors, the husbands and wives still chose their neighbors to be their *kumare* and *barkada* — the people with whom they would discuss family problems. It is clear therefore that husbands and wives turned to their neighbors for support when problems arose within the family. Sometimes, they confided in these neighbors instead of sharing problems with their spouses. Thus, in the same manner that they regarded these neighbors as confidants, they also found them to be a major source of stress and conflict. This phenomenon can be better understood if we remember that, in poor urban communities, the next-door neighbor is only a few meters away. In a sense, the neighbors take the place of the extended family, both as source of stress and of support.

On the part of the children, *pansin* (attention) was cited to be their primary and major concern. This is rather an unfortunate fact of life, for in a family situation like theirs, who else could still afford to give them the much-needed attention? In the same way, who could give attention to the mother or even to the father? Where could they possibly get the attention they all needed?

Aside from the need for parental attention, the children also reported the need for attention from other people. In talking about this, they were referring to the attention coming from the volunteer workers and student "tutors" who had regularly visited them. They further reported about feeling hurt *(nagtatampo)* when the tutors could not provide them the attention they craved for.

Pag-aaral came as a concern after *pansin*. Children viewed their eduction as their road to attaining a higher status in life or as a source of social mobility.

Magulang came after *pag-aaral*. On further elaboration reference to the parents meant marital fights, the father's philandering, drinking or hurting the mother physically — all of which the children were exposed to quite often.

To cite a specific case, one eight-year-old girl revealed seeing her father with his *kabit* (mistress). She further related that she did not inform her mother about it, lest her parents quarrel violently. In coping with the situation, she angrily confronted the other woman and told her to stop breaking up the family. The child took it upon herself to "carry" the problem and protect her family from the problem. Instead of misbehaving, which is more typical of children from higher-income families, this eight-year-old girl dealt with the problem promptly and directly.

In both high- and low-income families, however, the children act as "protectors" of the family. They absorb the stress and react to it in their own particular way. The child who confronted the other woman acted for the wronged parent and became her ally. But it would be wise to remember that, many times, the role of a family caretaker is too heavy a burden for a young child to bear.

The observation that poor urban children are more concerned with *pansin* is congruent with the results of a study by Naval (1979) on the coping and motivational patterns of children in poverty areas. Her study pointed out that while poverty and its varied forms of deprivation exposed the children to stressful conditions, the findings showed that the children were more preoccupied with improving their personal relationships.

As for the wives' manner of coping with their husbands' infidelity, one low-income urban wife revealed the same direct way of coping as did the eight-year-old girl. She went straight to the "other woman" and told her in no uncertain terms that, as an intruder, she was breaking up her family's solidarity. Interestingly though, she seemed to fail to acknowledge her husband's responsibility in this extramarital relationship. In this case, the couple's child did a drawing of the family where the father was depicted as the smallest and least developed of all family members. The father was also drawn without arms, implying an ineffectual and helpless figure in the family.

From other cases, it is interesting to note that wives from higher-income families dealt with their husband's infidelity in a different manner. They would either talk it over with a friend, relative, counselor, priest, lawyer, or even hire a detective before making any confrontation.

Putting all these observations together, the logical conclusion is that the marital relationship is still the pivotal point in the family. In all socioeconomic levels, it seems that a solid and strong marital relationship is the key to keep the family intact, especially in times of crisis. A pained marital union, on the other hand, is likely to be strained very easily, and all the more if extrafamilial stresses threaten the family solidarity. As Satir (1967), a noted family therapist, has so aptly stated, "The parents are the architects of the family." They are the builders and pillars that bind the family together.

The studies cited emphasize the need for improving marital relationships in concrete ways. It is very important for groups of people involved in this kind of work to consider the children's views as simultaneously interacting with their parents' views. Considering the views together gives a more complete understanding of the dynamics and functioning of the family as one unit, as one whole. In these troubled times, this approach could be of great value in strengthening and solidifying the Filipino family.

Further Discussion

This chapter has further underscored the need to look at the viewpoints of each family member, so as to understand how the family system works. The most striking observation is the way the spouses ranked one another as stressors: The wives noted their husbands as first among four stressors, while the husbands noted their wives as least among four stressors. Husbands and wives were both concerned with economic and community problems. Amid these considerations, the children are asking for more attention, or *pansin*.

In practice, family members differ in the way they perceive and state the reason for referral. This gives the therapist a very valuable clue as to why and how family members fail to understand one another. This issue is tackled further in chapter 4 and reflected in the intake interview form found in the appendix.

Another basic concept that this chapter brings out is that the marital relationship is important because it is the pivotal point in the family system. How a pained and bitter marital union has affected the relationships and families of subsequent generations will be more clearly illustrated in chapter 8. Strengthening and solidifying the marital union is a preventive measure, or initial step, in many cases of family trouble. How children cope with their parents' marital problems and some suggested intervention strategies will be tackled in the next chapter.

3

Helping Children Cope with Marital Discord and Separation

ISSUES CONFRONTING FILIPINO FAMILIES have been multiplying over the years. Some of the conflicts have to do with the differences in disciplinary methods between parents and grandparents, the question of power in the family, school problems of children, delinquent behavior, drug addiction, and the wide gap in educational attainment between parents and children — especially in the rural areas. One particular phenomenon, which has markedly increased in the past decade, is that of marital discord and separation. This continues to exert a tremendous influence on the stability or instability of the family.

The previous chapter clearly pointed to the marital relationship as the pivotal point in the family system. In this chapter, the problem of marital discord and separation will be approached from the child's own phenomenological viewpoint.

There have been many speculations regarding the effects of marital separation on children. The issue has grown to such a proportion that concerned parents have posed several important questions: Must we separate now or later? Is it better to stay together for the sake of the children? Are the children really affected by separation? How do we know if they are affected or not?

Unfortunately, hard research has not been done in this area in the Philippines. Owing to the sensitive and delicate nature of the subject matter, adequate time and serious effort are necessary on the part of researchers for them to obtain answers that truly reflect what children themselves think and feel about their parents' problems.

No published study, in fact, has looked into marital difficulties from the child's point of view. But considering that a family's problems — and the stresses they cause — are reflected in the behavior of its most innocent and helpless members (the children), it is but fair to heed their viewpoint regarding their parents' marital discord. It is important to know what the children's thoughts are about the situation. What are the children's feelings? What are their ways of coping and trying to understand the conflicts besetting their parents?

Some Intervention Strategies

To bring order into the discussion of some pertinent ideas related to marital discord and their effects on children, I have mapped out some intervention strategies.

First, I will try to see the situation from the child's own perspective, that is, to enter into the child's own world and to try to understand how the child makes sense of what is going on. I will also look into what explanations he or she tries to give in order to cope with the situation.

Second, I will cite some behavior or misbehavior of children who are caught in this situation. These behavioral responses will be seen as dynamically related to the marital stress. Corollary to this, I will present some nontraditional and innovative strategies that I have actually tried out in helping children and their families cope with this type of problem.

The theoretical orientation on which the understanding of the dynamics and treatment approaches are based is again the **family systems theory** (Andolfi 1979). As previously mentioned, the theory states that any stress undergone by any member of the family is inevitably experienced by all members of the family in some way. Andolfi further emphasizes this premise by stating that in the family systems approach, *the symptomatic behavior* — especially in a child — is a signal of some stress, or conflict, within the family system. Diagnosis is largely the assessment of the symptom's function within the family system, or what I would term as *finding the underlying message of the overt behavior.*

An important step in helping the child cope with the stress of his parents' separation is to begin from his or her standpoint, that is, to get into his or her feelings and perception, as if one is actually in the same situation he or she is in. Apart from this, the age and stage of his or her development are important factors that must be considered to understand how a child perceives stress.

How do children of different ages try to understand what is going on? Actual verbalizations by children of different ages have been captured in the following responses taken from interviews, stories about drawings, and play therapy.

A four-year-old boy said, upon drawing the female figure: "This is my mother, my other mother . . . because one is old and one is new." But his more articulate and very bright six-year-old brother seemed to feel it more deeply. He volunteered: "I have two mothers, because my mother is separated from me. My new father lives with my real mother. He is kind to me and does many things with me. I wish I could live with my real mother." Then the therapist butted in and asked: "Why can you not live with your real mother?" And the six-year-old boy answered: "Because she has to separate from me. Because she has a rumble-bumble in her head. I also have another father. Even when I am with my real father, I am also lonely."

The father (who is separated from his wife) of a five-year-old girl, came to visit the girl and the mother one day. When he was about to leave, the girl reacted by holding on to his legs tightly and imploring: "Say sorry, Daddy. Say sorry to Mommy and Mommy will also be sorry to you so you don't have to go away." This same girl constantly looked for the orphaned boy in her doll play.

An eight-year-old boy, trying to sort out his feelings, said: "Kasi naha-*hurt* ako, parang sumasakit sa dibdib. Kasi madalas nagagalit ang Papa ko. Umiiyak ang Mama ko. Natatakot ako kasi nagagalit at sumisigaw bigla ang Papa ko" ("I am hurt. It is as if my chest is painful. My mother cries because my father is usually angry. I am afraid because my father suddenly gets angry and shouts").

A girl of eleven expressed her feelings this way: "I get sad. I read, do my hobby — drawing — para makakalimutan (in order to forget). "Minsan natatakot ako, hindi ko alam kung bakit o kung saan." ("At times I am afraid, I do not know why or what about.").

Another eleven-year-old girl said: "I am lonely for my Daddy. He tells me about the good times we had together and I keep wishing we can get them back. My Mommy and Daddy should really get back together." (Many children of separated parents cling to the fantasy that their parents will reconcile — they cling to this fantasy even up to the age of eighteen.)

A boy of fourteen analyzed his problem cognitively and said: "It's better to separate because my mother has suffered already. My sister has a hard time because she was the favorite of my father."

From these examples, one not only gets a glimpse of the different ways children belonging to different ages or different levels of development perceive and feel the stress brought about by marital conflicts. More importantly, one also sees that each child, in his or her own way, exerts considerable effort to salvage, or make some sense out of the situation.

Aside from having a feel of the child's experiences, a therapist must consider as equally crucial the overt behavior manifested by the child, as well as some of the strategies used in helping him cope with his problems. Observations have shown that children who misbehave seem to be those who do not express themselves well verbally. In effect, they act out what they cannot say. Their behavior speaks more eloquently than their words. I shall cite five cases briefly to illustrate the intervention strategies I have applied, as the meaning of the behavior clarified itself while the treatment progressed.

Nightmares

Andy, a five-year-old boy from a musically inclined family, had nightmares accompanied by profuse sweating every night for one week. During therapy, he was asked to draw his dream. First, Andy drew an unidentifiable blob. As he continued to draw on one sheet of paper after another (fifteen pieces of paper were consumed), the blob gradually became clearer and became a monster. Finally, the blob became his parents fighting. When asked what he wanted to do with the drawing, Andy punctured the paper with several holes, crumpled it, stepped on it, and threw it into the wastebasket. It was as if he was exorcising the situation, at the same time experiencing some sense of power and control over it. (At the time he was drawing the blob, the therapist was right there along with him, drawing a blob on another piece of paper.) The parents later realized how much their son was reacting to their problem, and they decided to go into marital therapy.

After therapy, the mother was asked by the therapist to play soft, soothing music at bedtime. The week after that, it was reported that the boy did not have a single nightmare.

The series of events made the parents recognize that their son was very much affected by their fighting. And it finally gave them the jolting realization that they also needed to seek help for themselves. Consequently, the parents were seen together for some sessions. As expected, the boy was relieved of his problem.

The Family Barometer

This case is about Nena, the nine-year-old previously mentioned as the bed-wetter. She was the youngest of three children, her other siblings being a boy of twelve and another, a girl of ten.

The mother observed Nena's intermittent bed-wetting and could not connect this to any observable aspect of her child's behavior. She was doing well in school and just won a gold medal in swimming. She did not seem to have any other symptom, except that she was defensive and unwilling to talk much about her feelings toward her father. Later on Nena confessed she could not really control her bed-wetting. Thorough medical tests revealed no physiological basis for this eneuresis.

In trying to understand Nena better, the therapist administered projective tests to her. The most noteworthy revelation

in these tests was Nena's hostility toward her father and sympathy bordering on pity toward her mother. She projected a
father-image that was lazy. Later on, she verbalized that while
her mother worked very hard, all that her father wanted to do
was to play golf.

Further interviews with the mother revealed that the
frequency of Nena's bed-wetting periods coincided with the
negative relationship between her parents. The mother was
surprised to learn about this connection, especially because she
and her husband took care not to fight openly. They hid their
negative feelings toward each other when the children were
around. It seemed, however, that Nena was extremely sensitive
to her parents' tensions. Her sharp "antennae" picked up the
negative vibrations between her parents, even if they were not
overtly expressed.

Moreover, Nena was surrounded by a family of broken marriages. Her *lolo* and *lola* slept in separate bedrooms for years,
which eventually led to their separation. Her immediate aunts
also separated from their husbands, and she had an uncle who
simply refused to get married.

It is possible that, deep inside, Nena was afraid that her
parents' confrontations could lead to separation too. She might
have been nourishing fears that her parents would be the next
couple in the family to split up.

Given the case of Nena, one could ask these questions:
What could be happening in Nena's family? What role was Nena
playing? Looking at the dynamics involved, it would seem
reasonable to say that Nena was acting as the "family
barometer." Instinctively, she reflected the pressures of the
marital relationship even more accurately than anyone else
inside or outside the family could. Furthermore, her bed-
wetting served to direct the attention *away* from a possible final
confrontation that might lead to a separation of her parents, as
had happened to her aunts and grandparents. Through her bed-
wetting, Nena had at the very least channeled her parents' focus
to a common problem, that is, her bed-wetting. Marital therapy
was therefore the initial approach taken in the case. This was
followed by family sessions later.

The Slowdown Striker

A mother brought her ten-year-old girl for therapy and complained of her slowness in all her activities each morning. From the girl's eating to bathing, to dressing up, the mother was irritated no end by the girl's slow movements. "Parang nananadya " ("It is as if she wants to irritate me deliberately"), the mother commented.

Upon further probing, I learned that the child knew about her mother's discovery that her father had a current affair with another woman. The mother became very angry and had, since then, been fighting with the father.

As an initial step toward therapy, the child was brought in for a few sessions of behavior modification. Afterwards, the mother still complained that her daughter was the same "slowpoke." Further explanations and suggestions about easing up the pressures on the girl did not improve the situation. The whole family was then enjoined to come together for a session. The dynamics then became clearer after that.

The seating arrangement of the family members was revealing. This nonverbal behavior showed the division between the mother and the rest of the family. The mother sat at one end; the father, the twenty-one-year old *ate*, and the ten-year-old IP sat on the other end. Further observation during the family session showed the mother to be clearly domineering. She shouted and spoke in a loud, unpleasant tone of voice. The father, as well as the *ate*, explained how difficult it was to want to do anything when one was ordered about in such a manner.

In terms of therapy, one important discovery in the session was the fact that it was the *ate* who saw the division in the family and the assignation of her younger sister as the scapegoat. As a result, the *ate* was included in the therapy as the ***therapeutic ally*** and supportive person in the home. She helped by managing her sister's eating behavior and allowing the expression of her sister's pent-up feelings.

It was also necessary to explain to everyone, however, that the mother needed to be relieved of the task of having to monitor the progress of her ten-year-old "striker," lest she become the next family scapegoat.

The Lonely Girl

The eleven-year-old girl earlier mentioned, who felt lonely for her daddy, also said that she was ashamed to let anybody know that her parents were separated — except to her best friend, whose parents were also separated.

Seeing this situation, I asked the girl to bring along her friend for the next session. As a result, both girls were gradually sought to support each other in the therapy, without having to drag each other down in the process.

The Sibling Subsystem

This case refers to the family of the lonely eleven-year-old girl cited above. She had two siblings (both boys), one fourteen years old, the other eight. The girl was found to be oversensitive and irritable. It made her a crybaby. Furthermore, her grades in school had dropped.

In traditional therapy, the child with such a problem would be seen by the therapist regularly, while the mother would be asked to come occasionally. Using a family strategy, however, I asked to see the mother and the three children all together. A supportive sibling subsystem emerged as a therapeutic strategy.

During the therapy, the fourteen-year-old adolescent was observed to contain a strong controlled anger toward her father and deep empathy for her mother. Since he tried to deal with the situation cognitively, he was unable to express his feelings openly. He also tried to live up to the expectation that "boys don't cry" and, therefore, had to be as rational as possible.

The eleven-year-old IP was more emotional and often cried. The youngest brother, although fearful at times, was candid and spontaneous about the situation.

In such a family scenario, it became clear that the children complemented and needed one another to become a whole, therapeutic sibling subsystem. Each served the other with his own specific function. The controlled fourteen-year-old vicariously expressed his feelings through the emotional eleven year-old sister. The girl, in return, was helped to understand the situation more rationally by her *kuya*, while being spontaneous about her own feelings of confusion which were freely expressed in her many questions. The younger brother, on the other hand, felt safe — given the support of his *kuya* and *ate*. In effect, a built-in supportive sibling subsystem developed within the family through the therapist's use and reinforcement of the members' own individual resources. Each one had something to contribute and all three were made aware of this unique contribution. A more solid support system ensued from what was already existing in the family.

In order to be of concrete help to therapists and parents attempting to help children cope with marital discord and separation, I integrated those intervention strategies using the family systems approach, and came up with three pointers.

First. **The Identified Patient** (IP) must not be singled out as a problem child, or labeled as "abnormal." Rather, the child must be seen in the context of the entire family system. The message and meaning of the child's behavior can be uncovered and discovered within the dynamics of the entire system.

Second. It is important to be attuned to the child's total millieu and to the specific characteristics not only of the nuclear but of the extended family as well.

Third. All available resources within and outside the family must not be taken for granted. Rather, they must be harnessed and reinforced in the process of therapy. The existing resources, such as music, the friend, the *ate*, or the entire sibling subsystem can be utilized to the fullest with the aim of building the family's own supporting and therapeutic subsystem within.

As a further note, when one considers the anxiety and stress that accompany the process of separation, it is important to make the family members recognize their available resources and help them utilize these in order to keep the stresses manageable. Although the families may have been spontaneously using these support systems, they usually do so randomly and unconsciously. The processing of these dynamics in therapy is therefore still imperative, so that this built-in support system can clearly continue serving as an aid in supporting family members.

Further Discussion

An important concept brought out in this chapter is the creative use of human resources that are already existing within the Filipino family system. These available resources may lie dormant when they are not deliberately harnessed and consciously utilized. They may even become blocks to the coping process of family members. An example is the use of the *ate* as a therapeutic ally. Another is the utilization of the sibling subsystem as a built-in support mechanism. When each person's role and contribution to the coping process is explicitly spelled out to all, family members begin to appreciate and value one another, and at the same time recognize their own usefulness to the entire family. This give-and-take process must be made very clear for it not only results in a feeling of security derived from the support of other family members but also leads to an individual's sense of competence and self-worth that comes from being able to give something to others.

4

The Family Caretaker

I MENTIONED BRIEFLY in the previous chapter how children try to curb their parents' misdeeds by indulging in so-called misbehavior patterns. The cases summarized in this chapter serve as examples that clearly illustrate this phenomenon. They also show how this kind of caretaking can start at a tender age and that, most of the time, the family caretaker becomes the **Identified Patient** (IP). Following the general scheme of the book, the family therapy concepts are printed bold and are discussed at the end of this chapter. The next chapter deals with this "taking care" syndrome, but this time, among adult members of the family.

Renato: "I Want to Die"

Renato was referred to me because of his frequent screaming and crying. He also hurt his younger siblings and did not want to follow instructions in school. Apart from these, Renato was restless and had a very short attention span.

Renato was a good-looking five-year-old boy who was of average physical build. He was the second in a young family of four children, although he was the eldest boy. Figure 3, which is a genogram, depicts Renato's family composition and his **present living unit** (French 1977).

Although the *lola* (paternal grandmother) did not live with the nuclear family of Renato, she was in contact with his family almost every day. If she could not personally visit them, she would call them up by telephone.

Renato's parents got married quite early (at ages twenty and nineteen), thus making them financially dependent on the *lola*. Furthermore, both were unprepared for the responsibilities of parenthood. The mother was a housewife who had occasional jobs, like being a receptionist in a restaurant managed by her father. Renato's father, on the other hand, was an on-and-off businessman in his stepfather's firm that was run by his mother (Renato's grandmother). Hence, the father relied heavily on his own mother for his family's survival.

Moreover, since they mixed socially with well-to-do friends and acquaintances, they also felt they had to attend the same social functions and activities that this exclusive club — of which the *lola* was a member — attended. But certainly, they could not afford these socials on their own. The situation in itself caused frequent quarrels between Renato's mother and father. This same situation had also made the *lola* the power in the family. Figure 4 shows Renato's nuclear family.

While his elder sister was quiet and somewhat withdrawn, Renato was rather friendly, sociable, and outspoken. Renato was also observed to be very restless. He would constantly run around, climbing trees and walls. He was unable to sit down and concentrate on anything for more than ten to fifteen minutes. A neurological consultation showed negative results in relation to his hyperactivity.

A few months before the referral, I learned that Renato's family anticipated more financial burdens, as there was a possibility of losing their house because of mortgage and other payment problems. This event coincided with an observed increase in Renato's screaming, hurting, throwing of temper tantrums and negative tendencies, such as refusing to wear Physical Education (PE) shorts in school. At this point, there was also

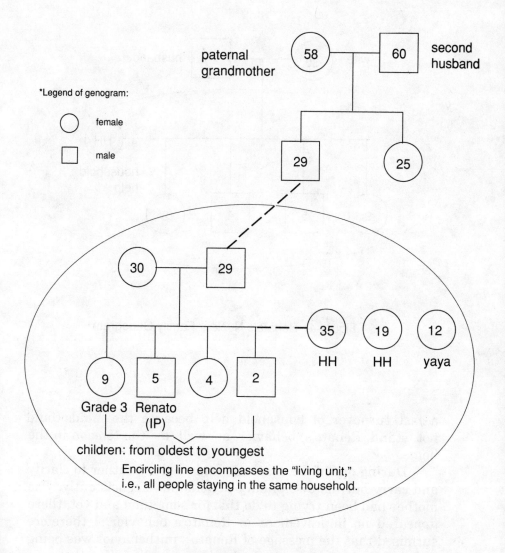

paternal grandmother

second husband

children: from oldest to youngest

Encircling line encompasses the "living unit,"
i.e., all people staying in the same household.

Figure 3. Renato's Total Living Unit

*This same legend applies to all the genograms in this book.

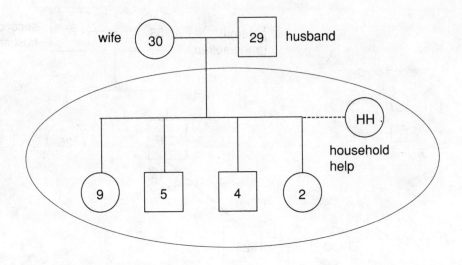

Figure 4. Renato's Nuclear Family Genogram

a fast turnover of household help because the maids could not stand Renato's behavior, as well as the tension in the home.

During one of the sessions, I advised the father to clarify and carry out his disciplinary actions more consistently. The mother had been trying to do this for sometime and yet, there appeared no improvement in Renato's behavior. I therefore surmised that the message of Renato's misbehavior was being directed to the father who had to exercise discipline that was firm and clear and, at the same time, provide much-needed assurance that he cared for his son. It was further explained to the parents that Renato's behavior was actually a signal — a call for attention — and that in cases like this, the behavior usually carries an underlying message. It was important to decode this signal to get its message.

Aside from inconsistent enforcement of disciplinary action, the parents constantly complained "life is so hard," without accompanying it with an assurance that, despite everything, they would still be able to tackle life's difficulties. This stance of the parents elicited a feeling of threat and insecurity in Renato who must have thought, "If my parents are not competent and adequate enough to conquer life's hardships, then what would happen to our family?" Although it is advisable not to shield children from knowing the harsh realities of life, their awareness of these realities must be accompanied by their parents' assurance that "Together, we will try and we can make it." This is especially true for young children, for if these constant sighs of despair are not accompanied by hopeful reassurances, the home atmosphere may turn heavy, depressing, and burdensome to them.

After looking at the *Gestalt*, or the whole picture of Renato's family, the logical intervention would be a combination of therapeutic approaches. My initial step was to see his entire family. This was followed by individual play therapy sessions with Renato. Separate sessions with his parents were also held. Toward the end, there was a session with the two *lola*, during which Renato's parents were also present.

Concurrent with all these therapeutic approaches, I undertook not only consultation with a neurologist but also conferences with Renato's teachers.

The heavy and depressing atmosphere in Renato's home was symbolically and graphically depicted during his play therapy sessions. Renato would fix the playhouse very carefully. Then, an earthquake would destroy the house. He would rebuild it again and again, asking the help of the therapist. But every time the house was finished, it would be crushed and destroyed by a hurricane, a flood, a typhoon, and other natural disasters. Renato's persevering behavior mirrored very clearly his need to set things right. At the same time, it also reflected his helplessness and powerlessness in the face of stronger environmental factors that his family could not control.

The therapy sessions were progressing when, one day, an incident clarified Renato's predicament. I had turned my back to get some art materials from an adjoining room, leaving my purse in the therapy room. As I turned around from the adjoining room, I saw Renato opening my purse, seemingly searching for something. When asked what he was looking for, Renato initially denied having looked into my purse at all. Later, he confided to me that he had tried to get a ten-peso bill from my purse. He explained that it was to be for his father's birthday and that he had wanted to make his father happy by giving him the money as a gift. His father had always been telling him that he had no more money.

Renato's explanation could be seen as an excuse to get off the hook, but I interpreted it as his way of helping his father. One day, this interpretation was reinforced when his parents frantically called me up for an extra session. They were in a panic because Renato told them that he wanted to die! During the session, I asked Renato why he wanted to die. He answered, "I want to die because when I die, I will be with *Papa Dios* [God the Father] and when I am in heaven with God, I will be very powerful. Then I can help my family on earth."

This heroic and touching revelation from a five-year-old boy brings out the message that was only too painfully clear — if Renato could alleviate his parents' sufferings, he would do anything, even to the point of dying for them! In reality, however, such a burden was too heavy for a young child to carry. Hence, his unusual behavior, which signalled the inner turmoil he was experiencing in his family.

In the therapy sessions I conducted separately for Renato's parents, one important focus was to develop their own sense of competence and efficacy so that they could more adequately carry on the vital task of parenting.

Rita: "Tatay Ko Pa Rin Siya"

Another illustrative case is that of Rita, a ten-year-old child prostitute. She is now in a rehabilitation house in a suburb of Manila, where I hold group therapy sessions. She lives in this center with fifteen other sexually abused children and three house-mothers. Rita has an eight-year-old younger brother, Tony. He is now in an orphanage for boys because their last surviving parent died a year ago. Their genogram (figure 5) shows the family composition.

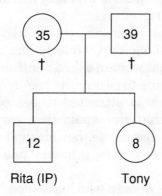

Figure 5. Rita's Genogram

Rita's mother died two years ago while her father died a year ago. The case study done by the house social worker revealed that Rita and her family constantly moved from one place to another since they had no house to live in. For several years, her family lived in an improvised house made of cardboard; it stood under a big tree along Roxas Boulevard, fronting Manila Bay. When it rained, they would take refuge in the building across the street. Her father was an alcoholic, and her mother would usually be out of the house supposedly to look for a job. They survived mainly on the money that Rita would earn by selling cigarettes. Sometimes her brother would tag along with her and she would then try to carry him while begging for money. She found out that people tended to give them money when they were begging together. Besides, who would look after her brother when her mother was out all the time and her father was always drunk? At night, there would be constant violent quarrels between her parents; and one day, she woke up to find out that her mother had left them. Rita and Tony tried to look for her but they could not find her.

After three months, she heard from other street children that her mother was very ill and was in a hospital. The mother needed money to pay for her medicines, so Rita tried to beg for money and was able to come up only with a few pesos. She brought these to the hospital. She stayed there overnight, trying to talk to her mother but she was very ill. She died the next day, before her father arrived.

Life for Rita became essentially the same (i.e., impoverished) until one day, while selling cigarettes, a woman approached her. That woman asked her if she wanted to earn big money without having to go out into the streets all the time. She told Rita that she was attracted to her olive skin and large almond eyes and that she would look very pretty if she was dressed up. In the meantime, her alcoholic father would push and nag her every day to earn money to support his drinking habit.

Rita joined the woman who had asked her and who then introduced her to three other women who were all dolled-up, and could have been into prostitution for sometime. The first night, after dressing her up, she was placed under the category of "play" which meant all the sexual foreplay without penetration. Later on, she was made to go through the total act.

For the next few weeks and months, Rita was relieved and pleased that she could earn money to buy good food for her brother and her alcoholic father. Her father stopped shouting at her since she was able to give him money every time he asked for it. The father would ask for money every day to buy his drink. In the past, when Rita could not give him any, he would scream at her and even beat her up.

After a few months, Rita was brought to the hospital because she had contracted gonorrhea. In that hospital, she met a woman doctor who enlightened her about prostitution and told her that if she went on with it, her sickness would recur. She then decided to visit a rehabilitation center for street children that offered soup and crackers to attract young girls. There she met a social worker who eventually brought her to the suburban rehabilitation house where she now resides. During one of the sessions, Rita said that what she really wanted to do was go to school and be adopted by a good well-to-do family. When asked why she had not simply run away from her father, she replied that she needed to take care of her father and her brother. She said that, after all, "Mahal ko siya, tatay ko pa rin siya" ("I love him, he will always be my father no matter what"). This kind of story is heard several times from abused children who still have to carry the burden of taking care of their families.

At present, Rita is in a residential treatment program where she has a full schedule of activities that includes group therapy, occasional individual therapy, moral education (taught by a religion teacher), and gymnastics. She is also learning to do such handicraft as macrame and quilting. She attends class every day with the other girls since classes are conducted in the rehabilitation house itself; a special education teacher goes there every afternoon.

Manolet: " I'll Work Hard to Support You!"

Manolet was a nine-year-old boy who was the younger child in a family of two children; his older sister was twelve years old. Figure 6 shows their genogram.

Manolet's father was a prominent obstetrician, and his mother was a refined and highly educated woman who was a creative homemaker. While Manolet was quiet, his sister was very outspoken. Manolet was brought in by his mother owing to his "low grades, lack of concentration—and he has been stealing money from us. At first he was getting only small amounts but lately, we were alarmed because he took three thousand pesos." Manolet's stealing a large amount of money jolted and alarmed his father, who was quite prominent in the community.

Notwithstanding his misbehavior, Manolet was described by his mother as very thoughtful and caring toward her. He was also observed to be quiet and well-mannered. His teacher described him as a nice and generous boy who was always ready to help his classmates.

Family history showed that Manolet's parents had been on a trial separation for one year now because of their frequent marital disagreements.

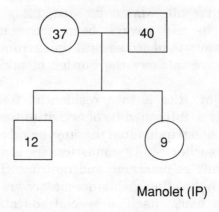

Manolet (IP)

Figure 6. Manolet's Genogram

It seemed that the husband needed to experience going out with others, and the wife told him to get his act together first. During this period, Manolet was very preoccupied with his thoughts and he would constantly check on his mother when he was out of the house. He would make phone calls from school to find out if his mother was safe. In his prayers, he would always ask God to make his mother happy and to make his father repent and come back and become a good husband to his mother.

Although the mother tried not to show it, her anger toward her husband was felt by Manolet which added to his own anger. One time he told his mother, "Mom, why don't you kick him or shout at him? He is being bad to you! When I grow up, I'll work hard to support you so you won't have to ask money from him anymore!" It seemed clear that Manolet was fighting the battle for his mother and was experiencing the hurt and anger that went with the fight.

The next intervention was a joint session with the parents to clarify and find out their stand regarding their marriage and to make them aware that they had to "pull their act together and make a decision which they could explain clearly to Manolet." A session with Manolet and his father also helped clear the air and a *regular* time together was agreed upon. Marital counseling sessions were also scheduled.

Further Discussion

Many times, the IP is the most sensitive and caring member in the family. He or she gets most affected, signals for help by becoming a behavioral problem, thereby falling under the label of "patient."

In the first case we cited, Renato was the brightest of all the children in the famly. His "antennae" were so sharp he was continually attuned to his parents' feelings, even if they did not discuss them in his presence. It is clear, therefore, that Renato's signal for help and his futile efforts in trying to help the family made him the IP.

It must be added, however, that there are individual personality characteristics that can contribute to one's becoming the IP. This is so because the IP may be the least intellectually endowed, physically the smallest, the least attractive, or have some physical or mental defect. These givens alone, however, do not constitute the total picture. The IP is somehow the one who is sensitive and attuned, and he feels the need to take care of his family, making him or her more involved than the rest of the family members. In the case of Rita, it seemed that there was no choice. She had to be the caretaker, being the *ate* in a family where the parents are unable to provide for their basic needs. In Manolet's case, however, he, being the quiet and sensitive one, had to do the acting out and the "taking care." The older sister was more verbally expressive. A thorough research study on who becomes the IP or what factors contribute to such a role will certainly shed more light on this phenomenon.

Without going further into the source of the phenomenon, the concept of the **Identified Patient** prevents the instant labeling of any one family member as *the* patient. The IP usually fulfills the function of sending signals that the family system is in crisis and, therefore, in need of help from outside sources. The following IPs, all children, were all trying to help their respective families by sending distress signals for more help: the seven-year-old boy who stole money from his classmates after his father lost his job; the ten-year-old prostitute who had to earn money every day to support her father's drinking sprees; and the six-year-old boy who refused to go to school after his father left for Saudi Arabia, so he could protect his mother from harm.

The *genogram* and the *living unit* allow the therapist to see instantly the family picture as a whole. For therapy, it is also important to include all members living together at the time of referral. At times, the maid, *yaya*, *lola*, or aunt (who may not be a member of the nuclear family) plays a very significant role in the Identified Patient's life.

That the child's behavior has an *underlying message* is another concept which helps family members see the need to decode the signal that the family is in a state of crisis or disequilibrium and, therefore, needs outside help.

For the therapist, counselor, or parent, a more detailed evaluation form for initial intake is given in the appendix.

5

The "Tagasaló" or "Mananaló" Syndrome

TAGASALÓ COMES FROM THE TAGALOG root word *saló*, which literally means "to catch." With the prefix *taga* it means "one who catches." Used colloquially, the word refers to one who "takes care, or one who comes to the rescue." *Mananaló* is a synonym of *tagasaló*.

A common tradition in Filipino childrearing is entrusting to older children the responsibility of attending to younger siblings. The eldest girl, or *ate*, and the eldest boy, or *kuya*, are both expected to have the authority and responsibility in the household next to the parents. More commonly, however, it is the *ate*, more than the *kuya*, who shoulders the responsibilities related to the household and family members. In the Filipino family, the girls are asked to help in the house quite early and are given a lot of responsibilities, while the boys are allowed to go out and play. This practice seems to have long-term implications in the children's adult life, as in their marital relations and work situations. Its relation to the *tagasaló* syndrome will be discussed later in the present chapter.

Guthrie (1961) has noted that, in both the urban and rural Philippines, the care of a six-month baby sibling was commonly entrusted to three- or four-year-old girls while the mother did the laundry or ironed clothes for a living. Although this is a laudable practice reflective of the dependable and supporting close family ties, it can also become compulsive, overgeneralized, and maladaptive if certain limits are left unrecognized.

Case Studies

There are times when the need to *saló* becomes unconscious, indiscriminate, and compulsive — leading to negative consequences for both the rescuer and the rescued. This phenomenon is expounded in cases presented in this chapter. After the case presentations, the dynamics of the *tagasaló* in the family context are discussed.

Tina, the Successful Lawyer

Tina, forty-one years old, was a successful lawyer. She was referred to me by an endocrinologist after a thorough medical examination produced negative results, except for evidence of high blood pressure. In Tina's own words, these were her chief complaints: "High blood pressure caused by tension. I need tension and stress management. Depression and debility during attacks caused by tension headache. Ulcers, back pain, feelings of nausea, heart palpitation, loss of appetite, going to the ladies' room, phobia of going back to work because of attacks, inability to manage tension due to demands of work and clients. Very negative thoughts supervene during depression. I am trying not to take tranquilizers . . . restless during waiting time . . . too many people distress me . . . feeling panic when alone in public places or busy areas."

This is one of the longest written lists of complaints I have ever encountered. It makes one immediately think of a hypochondriac beset with the whole gamut of neurotic symptoms — from phobias to compulsions, then to raw anxiety attacks. Another person might sum up these symptoms in one phrase — "burnt out." Somatizing, or getting sick, is the most acceptable way to take a respite without having to feel guilty. In Tina's case, it was the only way.

Recently, she reported feeling overwhelmed by the things she needed to do. Her niece needed money for her tuition, her associate in the office had to go on vacation and she had to take on his case load, her best friend was in a marital crisis and needed her shoulders to cry on, her husband was just recovering from his own bout with hypertension, she had a pressing deadline to meet, and so on went the list. To find time to take on all these concerns, Tina had been foregoing her lunch break for several weeks and was doing paperwork on weekends.

Objectively, the demands of her work were really great, and the needs of her relatives and coworkers were real. In other words, she was not imagining or exaggerating these at all. However, she assumed these responsibilities as if it was the most natural thing in the world to do. She did so unquestioningly and spontaneously, as if no choice was left for her at all.

With so many demands taking up so much of her time, Tina decided to ask for psychological help — mainly to manage her time better, and thus be able to fulfill all the obligations and duties she took upon herself without question or doubt.

At one therapy session, Tina recited all her burdens as if she were praying the rosary. Filling the air with heaviness, she ended her recitation by saying, "When I pray to God, I don't tell Him all my problems because He may become overburdened!" Such a statement revealed the height of her need to *saló*. She even unconsciously had to take care of God whom she believed to be all-powerful and all-knowing. Upon hearing her statement, I was prompted to tell her, "Sinalo mo na rin ang Diyos" ("You have even rescued God"). She then paused for a while and, for the first time, it dawned on her how deeply ingrained and compulsive her *pananaló* (taking care) was. She managed to laugh; but, sure enough, as soon as we were out of the therapy room, she was at it again. She told me, "I did all the talking and I did not even give you the chance to talk." It was only when I reminded her that she was doing *saló* of me (which she did not have to do) that she realized what she was actually doing.

Tina's case raises a lot of interesting questions with regard to the *tagasaló* syndrome. What kind of dynamics operates for the *tagasaló*? Is her behavior merely a conditioned response, a deeply ingrained habit which stems from early childhood upbringing? Or is the *tagasaló* a dependent person who actually needs to be taken care of, and is projecting (i.e., attributing) this need to others? Is her identity so uncertain that it needs to be maintained by the constant approval of others? How come she feels she has no choice about it? Where does the need to take care come from?

Perhaps we can better answer these questions through Tina's genogram (figure 7), which puts her situation in a proper context.

As shown in the genogram, Tina was the *ate* who had to take care of the household early, her mother being sickly. Although the mother managed the household, the father held the power (see chapter 9) in the family: he was the one who made the important decisions. When Tina was twenty-seven, her mother died. The mother's death gave her the additional responsibility of seeing after the legal papers of inheritance, because she was a lawyer. Having been used to taking care of the household, this came very naturally to her. Her doing *saló* began in this family, and gradually generalized to all the persons she came in contact with.

It was not until recently, after getting sick and being confined at the hospital, that she paused to question her role and decided to work this out in psychotherapy. As a result, she

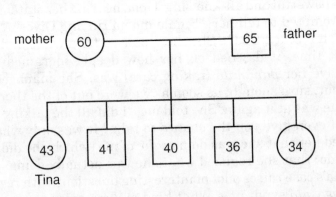

Figure 7. Tina's Genogram

learned to discriminate, prioritize, and say "no." Her somatic symptoms diminished, but she still needed to learn to be more conscious about her compulsion of automatically doing *saló* of everybody.

As in the case of Tina, it is generally believed that the *tagasaló* role is always assigned to the *ate*. The following examples, however, tend to put this hypothesis in question.

Nona, the Teacher-Businesswoman

Nona, a thirty-three-year-old teacher, ran a garment business in her house. She was the third in a family of six children. Her present living unit appears like this (figure 8):

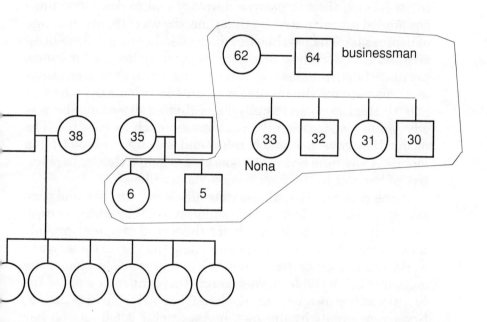

Figure 8. Nona's Present Living Unit

The *ate*, who was thirty-eight years old, left the house early to marry. With a brood of five children, she lived with her own family. The second sister, aged thirty-five, left for the

United States to take up courses and do some lecturing in universities. This second sister was a single parent with two children, a girl and a boy. She left these children (a six- and a five-year-old) with her parents because she was away from the country most of the time. She would visit her children anytime she wanted, and then leave them in her usual carefree manner. With her two sisters away from home, Nona eventually assumed the role of *ate* in the family. Living with her parents and the remaining siblings, together with the two children left behind by her elder sister, Nona virtually became the surrogate mother to her young niece and nephew.

Recently, Nona would become ill on and off for almost a year, and doctors could not diagnose her illness. She went to at least eight specialists in areas ranging from neurology to cardiology, then to gastroenterology and to dentistry, until she landed in psychiatry. By that time, she was already in a state of depression. The psychiatrist diagnosed her as manic-depressive and gave her a host of medications, which her good instincts prevented her from taking. After a long series of consultations and frustrations, she finally found an endocrinologist who was able to treat her successfully for a thyroid disorder. She was advised to avoid stressful situations as much as possible. The medication gave her much relief and she went abroad for a month. Away from home, she was able to gain a clearer perspective of her role in the family vis-à-vis her illness.

She realized that, all the time, like a real *ate*, she had been taking care of her elder sister's children like they were her own. She would buy them clothes, teach them good manners, provide them extracurricular activities and help them with their school work. On the other hand, her thirty-five-year-old sister, the mother of these children, was merely traveling in and out of the country at her own leisure. Realizing her sister's odd behavior, Nona wondered why her own mother never set limits on her elder sister's behavior, despite the fact that the two grandchildren were living with them. Nona further revealed that her *ate* had always been the "privileged one," treated like a princess from an early age. Since then, she had "never come down from her float," to use Nona's words. Her sister never had to handle the nitty-gritty at home. Her sister was the achiever. After obtaining her doctorate, she spent time lecturing abroad, while her two children (out of wedlock) were left to the care of her parents. Nona, however, did not want to displease her sister; besides she wanted to help her mother out, too. Although her mother obviously favored her elder sister, Nona never brought up the issue with her mother.

Since Nona loved the children of her *ate* very much, she naturally took to the task of rearing them. Aside from her nephew and niece, Nona also took care of her brothers, especially the thirty-two-year old, whom she once bailed out of jail. Since her two brothers were always out of the house and were not expected to help in the household, it was a younger sister who would occasionally help her out with the two children. Still, the bulk of the responsibility for their upbringing remained on her shoulders.

As mentioned earlier, it was only when Nona became ill that she began to realize that taking care of the family was a load she alone was carrying. She realized too that while she tried to take care of everyone in the family, no one even took time to look after her in the hospital. The family members could not and would not believe that Nona, the ever dependable one, could also become ill. She admitted that she could not break away from her *pananaló*, until she actually got hospitalized. This painful realization finally gave her the needed jolt to set limits for herself, and learn to say "no" so as not to get sucked in again. She understood that she was trying too hard to win the approval and affection of her mother, while her privileged sister did not even have to try — a fact she resented. She claimed she had to do the *pananaló*, for she did not know of any other way to find her place in the family and make her presence significantly felt.

Further reflection made her see that her compulsion, which initially began within the family circle, spread out to all the people she knew. In fact, she observed that all her friends who had sought her help in the past could not believe that she got sick. They always thought of her as a self-sufficient person who did not have to be taken care of. She noticed that she had always been quick to take care of people, leaving them no room to take care of her. As a result, it never occurred to others that she too needed to make *pasaló* (be taken care of). After sorting things out, she came to her senses and recognized that if she had not gotten sick, she would have just simply gone on and on in this manner.

Nona's example brings us to the issue of giving and receiving, which is vital if we are to understand better the *tagasaló* syndrome.

Fely, The "Burnt-Out" Housewife

Fely was a thirty-five-year-old housewife, with two sons aged seven and two. A counselor, she describes herself as "burnt out," having, in her own words, "to take care of everything in my life and only wanting to be taken care of myself." Her marital life was unsatisfying. She had the major role of looking after her two children because her husband was usually depressed by his job problems. She seemed not to feel any empathy from her husband.

The many stresses she underwent caused her to lose fifteen pounds, become nauseous, and feel weak constantly. She also suffered from loss of appetite and falling hair, which were part of her generally heavy and depressive feelings. Because of her own work as a counselor, she was more insightful about her own dynamics in the context of her family origin. Figure 9 represents her genogram.

Fely's mother was a housewife who was the queen of the house, running it the way she wanted, with a constant supply of household help. Although clearly the authority at home, she was helpless in times of crisis, when she would faint or feel weak, thereby needing to be relieved and rescued. Her father, a very prominent obstetrician, asked for achievement among his daughters. The real *ate*, aged forty-two, was, during her childhood and adolescence, the favorite of the father, who treated her like a princess. The mother subtly resented this favoritism, and this contributed to the *ate*'s early departure from home. This *ate* applied for studies abroad without letting her parents know. Her acceptance by a European university therefore surprised them. Only nineteen when she left home, she fully knew that her father valued career and academic achievement very much. The second elder sister, who now lives in Japan, had also left home immediately after college. She obtained a master's degree abroad; she comes back only for rare and occasional visits. Following the chronological sequence,

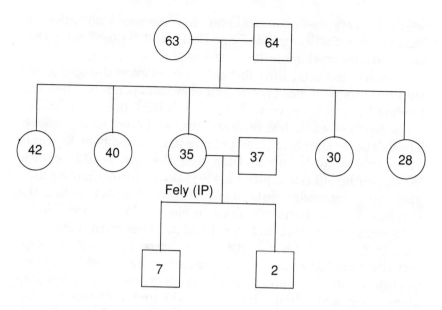

Figure 9. Fely's Genogram

the next one expected to leave the home would have been Fely, but she recalled not wanting to leave for some reason. She could not understand it then, but later she claimed that it was because she wanted to serve her parents. She did go abroad briefly to take some special courses in music, but she felt a strong need to rejoin her family in the Philippines. She came back and did the logical thing at that time — she got married. It seems this was also her mother's expectation of her. Fely obtained an M.A. in Guidance in the country, but she felt this was not enough for her father. (She felt strongly that, from the very beginning, her father had always wanted a son to follow in his footsteps — even if he was never openly demanding or pushy about it.) So she continued her studies toward a Ph.D., although she experienced a lot of difficulties while studying. In the middle of the course, she almost dropped out, not because of intellectual limitations but more because of her numerous responsibilities. At one point, she even toyed with the idea of shifting to medicine. Nevertheless, it was exactly during these times that she felt she had to go on. At the back of her mind, she knew that if she did not pursue her doctoral studies, her father would be very disappointed, and this she could not afford to happen. She finally finished her Ph.D. and "gifted" her father with a doctor in the family.

In her married life , she took care of everything, she felt that her husband was erratic and very undependable. She had to shop for groceries, drive her son to school and do numerous other tasks — while her husband was at home, sound asleep. The few times that he offered to drive his son to school, he would be unable to wake up in time and the son would be late. Whenever he offered to pick Fely and the children up from their visits to the grandparents' home, he would arrive so late the children would already be deep in sleep. Matters were made even worse by the fact that they lived in a suburban community quite a distance from the city. The exhausting situations kept recurring until they came to a point when Fely could no longer tolerate them. She moved back to her parents' home, bringing along her two children. She claimed she had to do this because she felt that she could no longer depend on her husband to do anything consistently. On the other hand, her husband felt that no matter how hard he tried and no matter what he did, it would not be good enough for her: she was always right while he was always wrong.

She further revealed that, by moving to her parents' home, she was actually looking for nurture; she had the need to be taken care of. But oftentimes, she would find herself taking care of the house, supervising her mother's maids when they were not doing their jobs well, and being attuned constantly to what her parents were thinking or feeling. Although her parents accepted her presence without question, she noticed she had to be on her toes to anticipate what they wanted from her, and yet never quite making it. It seemed no matter how hard she tried, she could never obtain the same degree of appreciation and affection her elder sisters obtained from her parents. Consequently, she found herself increasingly trying to please everyone she knew. Her need to please intensified until it became indiscriminate and compulsive.

When asked why she had to *saló* all the time, she answered: "Gusto ko ring magpasaló" ("I myself really want to be taken care of"). Yet, since she was always too quick to act to please others, people she related to did not get this message about her need. Somehow, she did not leave space for others to come to her rescue. She also confessed she sought out the caretaker role in the family and took it on wholeheartedly to have an identity. In other words, she needed to define herself in the family, so she could have a place in it.

While still hoping the adults in her life — especially her husband — would be emotionally supportive, she realized that her eldest son turned out to be the one doing *saló* of her all the time. Even at a very young age, her son had been very sensitive to her needs and tried his best to make her happy. At times when her husband would seem to unreasonably bully her, her son would say, "Never mind, Mom. Let's just be happy by ourselves." At a much earlier age, he even said, "Mom, just find a new husband. Anyway, you're pretty." Deep inside her, Fely knew her son was trying to carry her burdens. In effect, her son, who eventually became her *tagasaló*, picked up the message she had been trying to convey to the adults from whom she sought nurture.

This worried Fely because her son was too young for this kind of role. He had already begun giving signals he could no longer maintain the role. "Hindi ko na kaya" (I can't take it anymore"). (This is depicted in drawings in figure 10.) At one point, he acted out this internal problem by getting into all sorts of trouble in school. He resorted to attention-getting behavior and ended up being teased and bullied by his classmates.

In the son's drawings, he and his mother get knocked out and his father is "mad" and hurting others. Fighting in the family keeps on, with the father getting mad or hitting the mother and the children, while the mother "passes out." The son has taken over: "I was prepared with a stick with Mom gon [gone]."

The son of a mother who is a *tagasaló* turns out, in a lot of cases, to be the second-generation *tagasaló* of his own mother. This is especially true if the father is not meeting the emotional needs of the wife. This type of dynamics is similar to that operating in marital separation, in which case the son assumes the role of the absent father.

In Fely's case, her husband had been depressed for quite some time owing to dissatisfaction in his job. Consequently, he had been taking out his depression on the whole family, including the maids, by shouting, screaming, and at times, even by physically hurting them. On one occasion, while all these fits were going on and everyone was intimidated and afraid of the father, Fely's two-year-old— who was a very assertive boy— bit his father's leg. It was as if he had taken over the fight and come to the family's rescue. He was taking up the cudgels for them.

It was unthinkable for Fely to separate from her husband, because of her strong guilt feelings. She felt he was her responsibility on earth. She was stuck to the situation and believed she had no choice but to stay. With the husband's refusal to seek professional help, the situation did not change. In the meantime, the second-generation *mananaló* was getting overburdened. Given such conditions, how does a person distance

Figure 10. Noli's Drawing: Fighting in the Camper

himself psychologically when there is physical proximity? Is distancing really possible? At what price?

In the two preceding examples, the *mananaló* feels compelled and tries very hard to anticipate and "catch" people's approval and affection. Yet, there is always a feeling of not quite making it. Perhaps there is no substitute for a feeling of unconditional positive regard — a basic psychological need not even a Ph.D., or any degree for that matter, can fill up.

Yet, when the *mananaló* finally learns to get the approval from herself and gives it to herself, then she can start to let go of the unattainable and begin living her own life. She lets go of "trying too hard." This ability to keep a distance and differentiate on the level of the self is an important element in the treatment of the *tagasaló* syndrome.

Before going deeper into the dynamics and integrating family factors that characterize the *tagasaló*, two more examples will help focus on some finer points.

Lota, the Nurse-Psychology Student

Lota was a thirty-year-old nurse who was pursuing graduate studies in psychology. She was the second girl, but the sixth in a family of eight children, as shown in her genogram (figure 11).

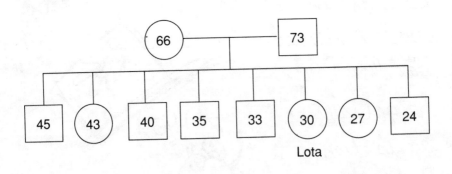

Figure 11. Lota's Genogram

The metaphor Lota used to describe her family was a "hanging mobile" because the family members were continually coming and going, which resulted in the family composition changing quite often. The "mobile" describes the situation aptly and captures the essence of the ever-changing and ever-balancing family system. As the composition changes, the system seeks a new balance or equilibrium (figure 12).

This given setup inevitably put Lota into the caretaker *(tagasaló)* role, until she became seriously ill.

Like the people in the previous cases, Lota did not pause to evaluate her role until she became seriously ill with an undiagnosed malady (it was suspected to be a liver disease related to a certain type of cancer). This really jolted her and gave her the necessary time and impetus to review her life in perspective. It was also during this period when her father became very ill, when her brother got into an accident, when her cousin was on the verge of death at an Intensive Care Unit, and when her nephew, her sister, and sister-in-law all became ill in turn. Being a nurse and a psychology student, she was much needed by all of them. She found herself fully involved in all these situations, catering both to her family's physical and psychological needs. In her own words, she said: "In retrospect, I became the TOTAL *tagasaló.*"

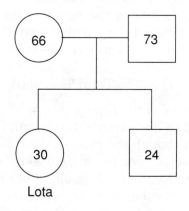

Figure 12. Lota's Present Living Unit

Without realizing it, she was becoming ill herself. Her taking care of others had finally taken its toll on her, but this realization dawned on her only when she was hospitalized. This was the only time she gave herself a break from taking care of the others without feeling guilty. Even more importantly, she was able to face the fact that she herself needed to be at the receiving end — to be taken care of, too.

Further probing revealed that she felt she had no choice but to *saló* all the time. "It went on and on. I felt that I was at the extreme *tagasaló* role. I tried to distance myself but I was also feeling my own helplessness to do anything about the situation."

Only when she became critically ill did she begin to listen to her body. It was also very painful for her to learn that the very people whom she took care of when they were sick (like her cousin) did not even find time to visit her at the hospital. This disappointment aggravated her illness. But it finally gave her the impetus to start setting limits, to learn to set priorities, and to say "no." Before this, she had thought of herself as having a "Messiah complex," which, perhaps, was actually her way of fulfilling her own need to be needed.

After reviewing these cases, a question like this could be raised: "Why did Nona and Fely get stuck to the *mananaló* role, while Lota could get out of it easily after becoming ill?"

The answer to this question becomes clearer when we look into the finer points among the *tagasaló* themselves. In order to make the distinction between the compulsive and noncompulsive tagasaló clearer, let us cite one more example.

Tita, the Total Therapist

Tita was the *ate* of the family. She was a psychologist who was very attuned to her parents' needs and feelings, even at a very young age. Although she was not the eldest, having a *kuya*, she saw herself as the "emotional caretaker" of the family. Her genogram (figure 13) gives a diagram of her family system.

Tita recalled that her mother, being the middle sibling in her own family where the *ate* was the favorite, was a natural and compulsive *tagasaló*. Tita strongly felt that her becoming a *tagasaló* had a lot to do with modeling after her mother. In

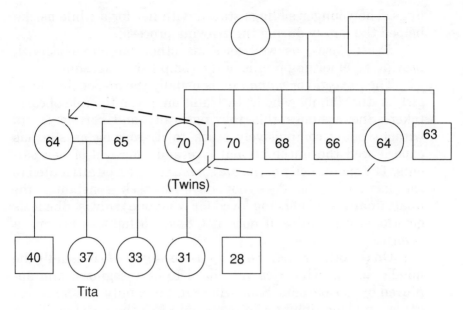

Figure 13. Tita's Genogram

Tita's case, however, she "embraced" the role of a *tagasaló* gracefully, and, at the same time, was able to set her limits quite easily. She was a noncompulsive *tagasaló*. Moreover, she became a therapist and, eventually, she became *tagasaló* too to her friends who found in her the inner strength as well as the technical skill and empathy they needed.

In Tita's family, however, the middle sibling, aged thirty-three, became the compulsive *tagasaló* and tried very hard to gain her parents' approval through academic achievement, becoming an outstanding student in the university. She also worked compulsively at her job, achieving excellence — almost to perfection.

It was very clear to Tita, however, that she was the favorite and she never had doubts about the unconditional love and approval of her parents. Tita, being the *ate*, never relinquished her role as the emotional caretaker of the family. When her parents and younger sister die in an accident, Tita and her own family became the anchor to her *kuya* and younger siblings. The younger siblings stayed with her for a while as she helped the family during the grieving process.

These cases, as well as some other families observed, provide an emerging profile of the compulsive *tagasaló*.

The *tagasaló* or *mananaló* is usually the *ate*, or the eldest girl in the family who is, by tradition, given the role of caretaker. She assumes this role naturally and carries it out without being compulsively stuck to it, so long as she has experienced the unconditional love and approval of her parents. The spontaneity of the *ate*'s *pananaló* can be attributed to the fact that she does not have to seek constantly the unattainable goal of being loved for what she truly is. She feels emotionally secure and does not have to fight to become a favorite.

On the other hand, the compulsive *mananaló* is usually the middle sibling who tries very hard to be recognized and approved by her parents. Somewhere in the family system is an *ate* or an elder sibling who is perceived as the favorite, like a princess who by birthright has gained a place in the family without even trying. The middle one, however, is still trying to find a place in the family and she never seems to feel the unconditional love of her parents, which is the foundation of basic trust and security (Erikson 1963). As a result, the middle sibling tries to gain recognition through achievement. She is usually anticipating other people's needs because she herself needs to be taken care of. In actuality, the message of the compulsive *tagasaló* is "Saluhin naman ninyo ako" ("Please take care of me").

Ironically, she finds it difficult to receive *saló* from others because she is so used to giving it automatically and unconsciously. Consequently, other people find it hard to fulfill her needs. Her message of needing to be nurtured is covered up by her own too-quick nurturing attitude and anticipation of others' needs. Thus, this person's compulsion is the result of a reaction-formation that covers up the real need both from others, as well as from herself. Somehow, this need that stems from lack of unconditional positive regard from the parents is never really met adequately, even if she continues to try very hard.

In therapy, the compulsive *tagasaló* needs first to see her place in her family in perspective. She needs to distance and differentiate herself from her family spectrum to become aware of the source of her compulsion and her underlying deeper need for unconditional acceptance. She is asked not to consciously and deliberately try too hard and not to seek to get this unconditional love from other sources. Transference and dependence on the therapist is often the first step. Without this family perspective, though, the therapist may also easily get sucked into a one-to-one dependent relationship.

Further Discussion

In the Filipino family, the female members are taught to be *tagasaló* early in life. They are expected to take care of household matters while the boys are allowed to play outside the house, so as not to get in the way. Starting from physical and concrete tasks, the female *tagasaló* moves on to take care of family members and parents emotionally. Somewhere in the development of her self-concept, the *tagasaló* is made to feel responsible for other people's feelings as well. A large part of her self-concept becomes dependent on her ability to please others in the family network. Her feeling of self-worth is tied up with the ability to make others happy. Because this begins at the early stages of development and is also at the level of the developing self, *pananaló* eventually becomes second nature and goes deeply into the unconscious vein. Since it is further reinforced very strongly by society, the role fits very smoothly and unquestioningly, for the inner need happens to be congruent with the external expectations.

Seen in the general context of Filipino society, the *tagasaló* syndrome is common among Filipino women. Very often, it seems a natural and endearing characteristic of them.

What happens to the male *tagasaló*? Since there is a *tagasaló*, there must be a *nagpapasaló* (one needing to be taken care of). Males are usually exempted from household responsibilities at an early age, yet upon assuming the roles of husband and father, they are expected instantly to be very responsible. What usually happens is that they need to be helped in coping with these responsibilities.

As a result, a complementary relationship takes place smoothly and unobtrusively. I have come across many women, however, who complain that the husband is very immature; he is often described as an eldest son. We do hear often of wives who jokingly complain that they have an extra child added to their actual number of offspring — the husband!

Lapuz (1977) discusses the problem in her book, *Filipino Marriages in Crisis*, with respect to the *querida*, or mistress, phenomenon. Jurilla (1986) further discusses the dynamics in terms of how the competent wife (among rural couples) have to defer to the husband especially in the area of sexual satisfaction.

Women's complaints in this regard are confined not only to the realm of marriage and the family. I have encountered many cases of women in offices who complain of their male co-workers acting like little boys. The women report having to boost the males' delicate egos all the time, else the men resort to attention-getting behavior. As a respected woman-columnist once told me: "I am amazed to see that these well-known personalities are really just like little boys acting out to get the attention of their mother." And yet, who does the mothering? The cycle goes on uninterrupted. A more systematic study of this phenomenon would yield important implications for Filipino parenting and childrearing.

It seems that the *tagasaló* or *mananaló* only stops to look at herself when she gets physically drained, ill, or burnt out. Otherwise, the syndrome goes on indefinitely. Doing *saló* can remain an endearing trait reflective of the Filipino's warm and supportive family system, so long as it does not become indiscriminate and compulsive.

Of key importance at this point is the awareness that the behavior of the *mananaló* is unconsciously determined. The realization that one has a choice to do or not to do so comes only after weighing the situation confronting her.

This leads us to a related and important concept in family systems, that is, the concept of **individual differentiation** within the family system. The need to distance oneself and see the family perspective as part of the therapy approach was mentioned earlier in relation to the use of metaphors (see chapter 1).

Historically, this concept was tackled by Bowen (1978) in relation to what he termed as the **undifferentiated ego mass**.

French (1977) later referred to it as the *"degree of differentiation."* Both Bowen and French considered it necessary for the individual to see himself or herself as independent from his or her family. Thus, a low degree of differentiation can be considered maladaptive or even pathological like the *"lack of boundaries"* in the undifferentiated schizophrenic.

However, this point is controversial because it carries very important cultural considerations. I have argued with French on the cultural implications of operationalizing this concept. To concretize my point, I isolate one diagnostic question found in the intake interview French used to get the individual's level of differentiation. The question goes this way: "Does she live with her family?" If a twenty-five-year-old married woman answered yes, to French this immediately implied *poor differentiation*. I explained to him that, in the Philippines, living with one's family of origin even after marriage is a rather common practice among women (as well as men). Given this cultural practice, can he therefore claim that these women have poor differentiation?

I am now reminded of Father Jaime Bulatao's metaphor of the hard-boiled eggs versus the fried eggs in a pan. The hard-boiled eggs refer to the Western mentality of individuality, which sometimes brings about alienation and loneliness. On the other hand, the fried eggs placed side by side in a frying pan depict the kind of togetherness among Filipinos. Although the yolks are separated, the eggs are still touching each other and are not totally closed or insulated from each other, unlike the hard-boiled ones (Bulatao 1981). I am tempted to add that an extremely low *degree of differentiation* could be likened to scrambled eggs in a pan.

It thus seems right to remind therapists who are helping individuals in the family that there is the need to keep the balance between aloneness and togetherness as suggested by the metaphor of the fried eggs in a pan.

6

The Special Child

IN FAMILIES WITH NORMAL CHILDREN, we have seen how one child usually assumes the role of the Identified Patient (IP) when the family is in distress. What happens to a family with a handicapped or mentally retarded child? Or families that have exceptional children?

In families where stress is built-in, some special adjustment is needed on the part of the family members. How the family members cope with a special child depends largely on the *family mythology*, i.e., their values and belief systems. Their manner of coping is also influenced by their perception of the special child in relation to their own self-image. How does a family with bright children, for instance, deal with a mentally retarded member?. What is the meaning of this child's presence in its members' lives? How do siblings deal with an autistic child? How do they make sense of his different-ness?

Our discussion will now shift to families who must live and deal with a special child. Four cases involving infantile autism, intellectual giftedness, mental retardation, and adoption will hopefully enlighten us on the many effects that such special children can generate on family dynamics and relationships.

How families eventually cope with these stresses brought about by the presence of the special child will be the focus of this chapter.

The Autistic Child

"Magiting" is the real name of a fair and very attractive boy who was referred to me by a pediatric neuropsychologist after initial assessment showed "autistic-like" behavior. He was brought to my clinic by his parents when he was only two years and nine months old. Just recently, Magiting turned nine. He is the second in a family of four children (figure 14).

Magiting means "brave" and, indeed, courage very clearly manifested itself in the boy, as he provided us the cues to follow on the therapeutic journey that led to his own "blossoming."

Besides describing the boy's courage, "magiting" is also the best word to describe his family, especially his mother — the consistent and dauntless person who became the key factor in Magiting's phenomenal growth and development.

This case illustrates how a family was guided to provide a therapeutic program at home, while therapy sessions were being conducted in the clinic. It also shows how an inter-

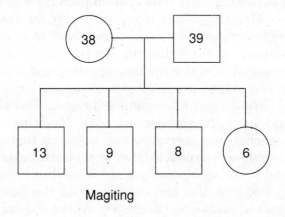

Figure 14. Magiting's Genogram

disciplinary team worked together on the IP's therapy. The neuropsychologist who gave him the initial assessment did follow-up testing every year as the treatment program developed.

Infantile autism is characterized by a pervasive lack of responsiveness to other people. There is gross impairment in communication skills — both verbal and nonverbal. This is evidenced by a child's mutism, delayed speech, immature syntax, and articulation (Rapport and Ismond 1984). Further, there is usually a peculiar speech pattern, a preoccupation with objects, and a ritualistic, compulsive behavior that resists change.

During the first year of Magiting's therapy, individual play therapy sessions were conducted weekly in the clinic, while the parents were given a regular, systematic, and daily program to be immediately conducted at home. The parents were also seen weekly to monitor the daily home program, point out the small gains made by Magiting, and plan the focus for the coming week. These sessions not only helped Magiting improve but, most importantly, they also helped the mother to persevere even when improvements seemed to slow down. The emotional support and the professional guidance the mother got during these sessions were crucial to maintain her consistency and persistence from day to day, week to week, month to month, and year to year.

The total therapeutic intervention package was especially designed for Magiting, there being no center for autistic children in the Philippines. The package consisted of an improvised team consisting of the following professionals: a pediatric neuropsychologist who did the neuropsychological assessment every year and helped guide Magiting's educational program; the clinical psychologist who conducted regular individual play therapy and later group sessions with Magiting; a special education teacher in a special school; a speech therapist; and, later on, a regular classroom teacher and a principal of a regular school. Besides seeing Magiting and his mother regularly, the clinical psychologist also had sessions with the family or one of its members when deemed necessary. As the clinical psychologist, I also contributed toward designing the educational program and recreational activities of the family.

The mother, with the constant support of the father, formed the essential core of the therapy team. Aside from planning outings and such activities as swimming lessons for her children, she also conducted the regular therapeutic program at home. The mother coordinated the efforts of the therapeutic team and arranged all the team and school conferences. Eventually, Magiting's parents formed a parent group with others who also have autistic-like children. Midway in the therapy, Magiting's mother took him to the New York Center for Autistic Children. There, Magiting underwent a comprehensive medical evaluation, including some medication that was later found to be unnecessary. (The details of a therapy program for autistic children will in the future be presented in a separate monograph on therapy for autism.)

The mother narrated she first noticed something different in Magiting when he was one and a half years old. Being a very attractive baby, he was entered in a baby contest and ended up as one of two finalists. When the interviewer gave the instruction, "Go to the chair and bring what's on it to me," the first baby followed both instructions but Magiting simply walked toward the chair and stood there with a blank expression on his face. The mother said to herself, "There is something wrong." Because Magiting could hardly answer when his name was called, he was thought to be deaf perhaps. He was brought to an eye, ear, nose and throat (EENT) specialist for examination, but the doctor could not find anything wrong. At this point, the mother heard of a neuropsychologist who had just arrived from advanced studies abroad. To him the mother brought Magiting for evaluation. The neuropsychologist diagnosed Magiting as "autistic-like." Upon hearing the diagnosis, the mother broke down and "cried and cried." She felt her son had "something terrible" and asked the neuropsychologist to explain to her what the disorder was.

When she reached home, the mother discussed the diagnosis with her husband. Although still heartbroken, she remembered a statement of the neuropsychologist — "Magiting could improve; he could learn and be near normal." The mother and father started to question themselves: "Why did we get a son like Magiting? Is his illness hereditary? Did we do something wrong to deserve an autistic child?" Her husband comforted her by saying they would study and learn everything about autism. In the meantime, they would focus on helping Magiting. It was during this period that they came to me for therapy, and they have consulted me regularly since then.

At the time of diagnosis, Magiting had two brothers — Dakila, who was eight, and Marangal, who was only one year and nine months old. It was Dakila who asked why Magiting did not talk. He also speculated that "maybe he is from outer space." Apart from this, Dakila seemed to be the least affected by Magiting's condition, probably due to their wide age gap and his position in the sequence of the children's birth. While Dakila played with other children, Magiting always played alone with puzzles and coloring books. By the time Magiting was three, he was enrolled in the same Montessori school that Dakila attended.

At home, however, it was observed that Magiting was quite negative toward his younger brother, Marangal. He would leave the room whenever he saw Marangal with their parents. At times he would pull at Marangal's hair. He was disciplined for this misbehavior. For a while, Marangal was very patient with Magiting, but, gradually, Marangal became withdrawn and began losing his self-confidence. Toward the end of the first grade, Marangal claimed, "I don't think I can go to grade two; I can't make it " — this notwithstanding the fact that he had been among the top ten in class. Marangal's attitude could perhaps be attributed to the attention given to Magiting, which deprived Marangal of what he needed at that stage of his development. Dakila, on the other hand, took Magiting's case positively and gladly remarked, "Magiting is a celebrity in school." He was undisturbed, inasmuch as he was older and had a peer group of his own. This was not true in Marangal's case. Being only a year younger and the target of Magiting's hair-pulling and pinching, Marangal could not assert himself and find his own place. He also sensed that Magiting was special and that it might be wrong to hit back. To top it all, he got a baby sister when he was about three years old. Marangal did not even have enough chance to be treated as the youngest, or *bunso*. A few sessions were held with the parents to enable them to give Marangal more systematic attention and assurance, so he could assert himself. Marangal eventually recovered, found his own peer group, and became closer to his eldest brother and father.

Mayumi, the baby girl, was only two when Magiting and his mother left for the United States. This was another difficult and traumatic event for the family, as the mother was heartbroken to leave her husband and the other children. At four, Mayumi got worried and started to ask revealing questions like, "Mommy, what will happen to Magiting when he grows up? Do I have to take care of him?" Mayumi, though the youngest, seemed to be drawn toward becoming the *mananalo*, as described in the previous chapter. This might have to do with her being the only girl, and with her seeing how her mother was taking care of Magiting and all the rest of them. It is commonly observed that siblings often take the role of parents' aides or supports, identifying with the special concern for the special child's well-being (Adams 1971). The eldest girl is usually assigned the role of caring for the afflicted sibling. In this case, however, the youngest seemed poised to assume the role, perhaps because she was the only girl.

Looking back at how Magiting's family coped, it appears that the mother assumed the key and central role but had the support of her husband and family. The entire extended family helped her as well. Her own mother not only gave her moral support but even paid for Magiting's therapy sessions. The other *lola*, the paternal grandmother, took care of the children when their mother was away. The aunt, who was Magiting's godmother, gave him attention and financial support. Another aunt helped him get to New York and stayed with them at the Center for Autistic Children. Second-degree aunts and uncles, as well as cousins, gave their assistance because they were part of a very closely knit extended family. Hence, aside from the work of a team of professionals, the all-out moral and financial support from the extended family greatly helped Magiting's family cope in a special way with this special child.

At the time of this writing, Magiting has been mainstreamed. And he goes to his special school only for swimming and other physical-social activities. He communicates verbally in an almost normal manner. Except in mathematics where he is rather slow in improving (due to the persistent delays in his abstract concept formation), Magiting is doing as best he can in his school subjects. He is also quite able to relate effectively with others. His ability to relate to persons is shown in his drawing (figure 15).

In contrast with Magiting's case is that of another autistic boy, Victor, who is now five years old. Victor is the middle child in a family of three children. His family picture is reflected in figure 16.

Figure 15. Magiting's Drawing

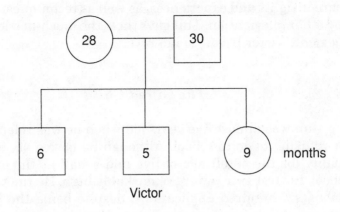

Figure 16. Victor's Genogram

The development of Victor was very much hampered by an intense sibling rivalry between him and his *kuya* even before the youngest, a girl, was born. His *kuya* was extremely aggressive to the point of hurting and intimidating him. When the two brothers were together in group therapy with other children, Victor would hide under a big pillow the whole time. This Victor did not do when his older brother was not in the playroom. It became clear that Victor was bullied and intimidated by his brother, so much so that he could not continue to "blossom."

The family situation was further aggravated by the birth of the baby girl. In this case, therapy for the *kuya*, concurrent with family therapy, was needed. Coping for the family was difficult because extended family support was not readily available. The young couple had to carry the burden of their special child all by themselves.

In this case, the parents were given regular guidance and emotional support. Aside from this, Victor was included in my group therapy sessions with five other autistic children. These sessions were conducted weekly with five assistant therapists using a one-to-one interactional model in a group setting.

At the same time, I met with Victor's parents together with the other parents whose children were in the group. The parents formed their own small group in which they could share insights and experiences, as well as techniques, readings, and other information. This gave them the much-needed encouragement. Victor began to improve.

The Gifted Child

Jun was almost five years old when he was referred to me for refusing to go to school. Although he lacked six months to qualify for the cutoff age of five and a half at the opening of school, his test scores were remarkably high. He ranked second among six hundred applications, despite being the youngest. Because of this, his parents requested that he be admitted to the Prep program in an exclusive school for boys. Figure 17 (the genogram) shows the composition of Jun's family

Jun's parents were both medical doctors who were busy most of the time. The eldest brother who was in the seventh grade was silver medalist at the same school that Jun attended. This brother had a special disability that had to do with his bone structure. He could not walk and had to move around in a wheelchair. Despite this disability, he was always among

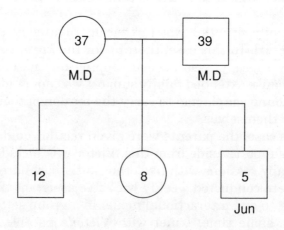

Figure 17. Jun's Genogram

the top three of his class. Jun's sister, the only girl, was a gold medalist for her academic achievements in an exclusive girls' school. As for Jun, he was observed to be gifted even at a very young age. He had excellent concentration and could get absorbed in a task for more than thirty minutes at a time when he was only one year and seven months. He was extremely observant and would ask amazing questions; when he himself was asked questions, he could give equally amazing answers.

He seemed to like school during the first months of the schoolyear. He attended classes very regularly. But by the time the second quarter came, he told his parents he did not want to go back to school any more. The parents poked around, trying to find out the reason for Jun's decision. Was he bored? Or physically exhausted? Did he fight with a classmate? Did the teacher shout at the class? Was there a bully in his class? Was he in fact too young to be pressured in a competitive school which had demanding academic standards? Did anybody in the family recently leave or die?

None of these common causes for children's refusal to go to school seemed to have influenced Jun's decision to stop schooling. When I saw the family together, the interaction among them was pleasant and there did not seem to be any underlying resentments or fears.

Alone in the playroom, however, Jun became very restless. He moved about and jumped nervously when asked any question regarding school. When asked to do any task, he was very cautious, critical about his work, and tended to be a perfectionist. At the therapy session, he was reassured that whatever answer he gave would be okay as each child might have an answer different from the others. He was further given the assurance that it was all right to make mistakes and it is "only God who does not make mistakes."

The parents, whom I met with as a couple, were asked to give an idea of a typical day in their home. Everything they narrated seemed quite ordinary until they began talking about dinner time. Apparently, as in ordinary families, they had discussions at the dinner table. Further probing on the kinds of questions they asked during dinner time showed these all had to do with academic achievement. Often they would ask: "How's your math?"; "How are your grades?" When once Jun showed his parents an exam paper with a grade of 97, the mother looked at it, turned to the error, saying, "Why did you make a mistake here? I am sure you know the correct answer but you were just careless!"

Unknowingly, the parents had given Jun the message that the grade of 97 was not high enough for them. He had no reason or no business committing any mistake because they all knew he was very bright. The parents' perfectionistic expectations were now subtly and unconsciously weighing heavily on him. (After Jun's play therapy sessions, however, he would go home lighter and happier. In fact, when asked about mistakes, he retorted, "The doctor said only God does not make mistakes.")

I had one more session with Jun's parents, mainly to make them aware of their subtle but strong pressures on the child. They were told that Jun did not want to go back to school because he was afraid to commit mistakes. Some simple and concrete steps were suggested to the parents. They were asked, for instance, to vary their questions about Jun's school experiences. They could ask Jun about his friends or his physical education class.

The parents were also given a framework to guide them in the total and well-rounded development of their child. The guide was in the form of a checklist which made sure that equal attention be given to the developing child's physical, emotional, social, intellectual, and moral needs. Such a framework is especially important to the development of the gifted child, so that he or she does not grow into an "intellectual monster" who is emotionally retarded, morally undeveloped, or worse, immoral. Intellectual brilliance is an asset or a treasure, but if this is not developed in the context of the total person, it can be used for immoral and selfish ends.

This case illustrates how parents can unknowingly and subtly impart a message regarding their expectations. This is so natural and so easy to fall into, especially if the child is intellectually gifted. It is equally easy to spontaneously focus only on the child's intellectual aspect and neglect his or her social, emotional, moral, and physical development. Effects of this lopsided development are evident among many adults in our society today.

Parents of gifted children have often described their predicament as both a blessing and a burden. Although it is their pride and joy to have a very bright child, they realize it takes more than just "ordinary parents" to handle a precocious child.

Take the case of Benjie, now six years old. He was the youngest among three boys — all intellectually gifted. Their parents were both doctors, both prominent in their own fields of specialization and were — necessarily so — both very busy. Benjie seemed to have the predicament of an only child, because his two brothers, aged nineteen and seventeen, were much older, and both were in college. Most of the day, therefore, he would be alone at home especially early in the afternoon.

Benjie showed signs of giftedness at an early age. At the age of one and a half, he could concentrate on a task for almost an hour. He would sit down and draw, label his drawings, and make stories about them. He learned to read the alphabet and count before the age of two. One problem then was that he would get very frustrated when he could not draw a star or the letter "A" very well as his muscles were not yet developed for fine writing. The whole morning, he would read books with his *yaya* with such intense concentration that his mother had to divert his attention and make him play with the animals in the garden. Another sign of giftedness was his extreme alertness to whatever was going on and his ability to express this in symbols. The drawings below (figures 18 and 19) exemplify this alertness.

Figure 18 is a drawing Benjie did when he was but three and a half years old and was attending nursery school. His mother was not home and there was no phone. He wanted to tell her about a distressing event that happened between him and the *lavandera* (Aling Ola) — and he posted the drawing on his Mom's bulletin board.

Benjie had just been listening to, among other things, the talk about the brutal killing of a TV personality, when he went up and posted a drawing (figure 19) on the wall where the other family members would surely look. It tells the story of a boy who loses at first but eventually wins in the end. The feeling expressed was that of having overcome an obstacle.

Benjie asked questions incessantly: "What's light made off?"; "Why does *lola* like one *kuya* more than the other *kuya*

Figure 18. Benjie's Drawing: Benjie and the *Lavandera*

Figure 19. Benjie's Drawing: The Boy
Who Wins in the End

when he is not good most of the time?" One difficult decision for the family to make was whether or not to send him to nursery school at such an early age. Since he was delicately built — and he still needed to take some sleep in the morning and in the afternoon — the parents did not want him physically taxed and strained. They therefore decided to try the nursery school not far from their home. It turned out that the teacher there was not stimulating enough such that Benjie quickly lost interest in going to school and did not want to go back any more. The parents did not force him to. Benjie's parents' problem of finding the right school for a gifted child is a common problem among parents, especially when the child is ready for formal schooling.

Benjie's *yaya*, who was intelligent enough to keep him stimulated, left when he was about four years old. When Benjie — just about five years of age then — was already in prep school, he developed a full-blown crush on the family cook — a bright nineteen-year-old girl who was good at playing with him. It was not an ordinary crush. Once in a while when not at home, Benjie would stop what he was doing and think about her. He would wake up at five in the morning to help her set the table. He wanted to kiss and caress her most of the time and to demand that she kiss him in return. This was not a very unusual demand, since the show of affection was very natural and profuse at home. The parents were openly affectionate to each other and the children. Benjie's "love affair" became a problem because the maid could not bring herself to be affectionate toward Benjie. She was either not used to it or she felt his advances to be more than "childlike." The problem became too much to handle, so the maid was dismissed.

Although the parents were affectionate, they did not seem to have enough time to be with Benjie at such a critical time when he needed both affection and stimulation. The mother herself decoded the underlying message of Benjie's behavior: the child needed more regular time with her or her husband; that underneath all the child's precocious behavior was a real need for stimulation in all aspects — intellectual, emotional, physical, and social.

Benjie was made to join a group of gifted children that met every Wednesday. He went to his mother's office, which was a

child center, on Mondays and Fridays. He also had regular
tennis lessons on Wednesdays and Sundays, which he enjoyed
tremendously. His father would eat lunch with him on Satur-
days and take him out. His older brothers were also put in charge
of playing with him, reading to him or just being with him on
Tuesdays and Thursdays. Although his regular school was
demanding academically, Benjie needed more than that chal-
lenge. When this need for stimulation was not met by the family
members, Benjie sought and demanded it from the maid — the
one who was most available.

Intellectually gifted children have a greater need for
stimulation and will usually demand this in some way. It is
important to distinguish this genuine need for stimulation
from a simple demand for attention, which could lead to self-
centeredness.

The Mentally Retarded Child

It is commonly said that a retarded child is viewed uniquely
by the Filipino family. Having a retarded child is often regarded
as a "good luck" sign — a gift from God. The retarded child is
supposed to bring good fortune to the family, especially in
business. It is also believed that the family, by virtue of having
such a child, has "paid its dues," and has its cross to carry. Thus,
they will be spared of other misfortunes.

Although such thinking may help the family cope with
having a retarded child, it may prevent the further growth of the
child himself, since it lessens the probability of the child's
receiving professional help. He gets no systematic program for
improvement.

While some families may consider their retarded child as
one who brings good luck, this is not true of other families.
Ultimately, the attitude toward the retarded child depends
largely on the family's collective self-concept, especially the
parents' self-image. In providing help to a family with a retarded
child, the therapist can be guided by the realization that the
child cannot be viewed apart from the total context of the family,
that is, its values, attitudes, self-image, and status in the
community. After all, safeguarding the family name is still an
important value among Filipino families.

The following case illustrates how family attitudes affect the development of a retarded child.

Emma is the eldest *(ate)* in a family of four children who are all girls. Figure 20 is a diagram of the family picture.

The father has his own business to manage, while the mother is after her Master in Business Administration degree. The mother is a bright woman who happens to be an achiever.

Emma's parents first came to ask for help for Emma when she was twelve years old. They had observed her to be slow and unable to cope with regular schooling. Initially, Emma was given a comprehensive psychological evaluation, which revealed moderate retardation. It was recommended to the parents to send her to a special school for mentally retarded children, and this was to be supplemented with group play therapy. They were further asked to do a stimulation program at home and have Emma enrolled in some skill courses, such as typing, cooking, and the like. Although the parents took Emma to attend the play sessions, they dragged their feet in terms of her schooling and skills courses, which were the more important parts of the therapy program. In fact, they did not even bother to look up the special school recommended to them.

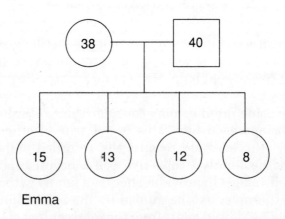

Figure 20. Emma's Genogram

Hoping to achieve some progress, I reminded the mother as often as possible regarding the recommendations. The mother was quite evasive. She would leave Emma in the clinic and pick her up as quickly as possible. This went on for sometime. I later gathered from Emma that she was usually left alone at home the whole day, while the rest of her siblings went to school and her parents went to work. I again reminded the mother emphatically about Emma's schooling; she replied that her relatives, especially the grandparents, would not approve of it. They would say: "Bakit mo pa papapasukin sa eskuwela? Pareho din naman. Sayang lang. Ganoon din yun" (Why send her to school? It would be merely a waste. She will not change anyway.")

There was, in the extended family, an atmosphere of resignation and hopelessness. The general feeling was that, since Emma was retarded, there was no use wasting time and money on her. That schooling for her would just be futile.

At this point, I insisted that Emma be enrolled in a special school. Knowing she would go on a tantrum when not brought to the play group, I used this as a leverage. I told the mother that if Emma was to continue in the play sessions, then she had to be enrolled in a school which she could attend regularly. Emma would continue to be relegated in the background and forgotten had not the threat been made.

In contrast, Norma, an adopted child aged seven, was referred by the adoptive mother after a comprehensive neuropsychological assessment revealed mild retardation. Norma was the younger of two children — the older one being a boy of nine who was doing all right in school. He was also an adopted child.

The mother came to ask me how she could help Norma improve in any way possible. She confessed she might have contributed to the problem by calling Norma *boba* (stupid) every time she tried to tutor her. At that time, Norma was attending a regular Montessori school allowing individualized instruction, that is, working at one's own pace. The mother also wanted to know if the IQ was a permanent score. Whe she was told it could be improved to a certain extent, she became very motivated to do all she could for her daughter. She started to refrain from calling Norma *boba* or any other derogatory term.

She even considered hiring a tutor trained in special education. Moreover, Norma took up art lessons and joined group therapy sessions, which helped her greatly in expressing herself and in boosting her self-confidence.

After one year of this intensive improvement program, a follow-up evaluation revealed an IQ that was ten to fifteen points higher (this placed her very close to the low average category). The mother exuberantly reported how she had discovered that Norma was not stupid after all, for she did well in school and her self-confidence blossomed. She also became physically more attractive.

The Adopted Child

What makes the adopted child special? How do family members cope with the child's presence? How is it that the adopted child behaves differently even when, as adoptive parents claim, he or she is treated in the same way the natural siblings are treated?

Mandy, ten, was adopted by a family after his real mother left him to their care. The mother, who came from the province, could no longer afford to rear him.

From the very beginning, Mandy had an extremely difficult time getting a sense of belonging in the family. A single look would tell anyone that Mandy was thin, dark, and small, while the rest of the family were tall, fair, and stocky. Apart from the physical contrast, the other children were all achievers, getting awards for academic excellence in their schools. Mandy was, on the other hand, at most only average in IQ.

The family genogram is given in figure 21.

The mother was a brilliant mathematician, and the father was a well-known lawyer. The twelve-and seven-year old boys went to an exclusive boys' school, while the five-year-old girl went to an equally exclusive school for girls.

When the adoptive parents first came to see me, they had several complaints about Mandy. They claimed that the boy, who was enrolled in a community school near their home, was flunking some subjects. He did not come home immediately after school, but stopped at a nearby store and chat with

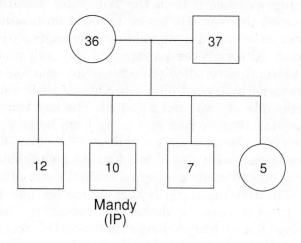

Figure 21. Mandy's Genogram

group of men. He had also been caught getting money from his brother's piggy bank. The parents wanted to know whether Mandy could not really tackle schoolwork owing to limited intellectual potential or was just emotionally disturbed in adjusting to his new family life.

The initial evaluation showed Mandy had an average IQ, with some below-average scores on verbal subtests (that actually needed reinterpretation in the light of certain cultural biases). Given optimum emotional and social support, he could pass his subjects without too much difficulty.

When interviewed, Mandy articulated his problem. "In the province I was bright. Now, I'm not bright any more." This very clearly reflected a feeling of losing his sense of competence and confidence, as well as a feeling of dislocation in his new family.

At the time the sessions ended, Mandy's sense of competence, which initially stemmed from his talents in biking and running, had increased because of many other newly acquired skills. Even his academic performance improved noticeably. And just before his therapy ended, he told me, "You know what, I'm bright *na!*"

Nothing was heard from the family for sometime until Mandy turned thirteen. He began to insist on looking for his real mother so he would come to know why he was given away for adoption. Although the parents did not seek professional help any more, they handled the issue in an open and straightforward manner by trying to reassure him of their continuing support. But Mandy was not satisfied. The last thing I heard about him was that he had run away from home to go back to the province, looking for his mother. He never found his mother for he met with a fatal accident before he could.

This is an extremely tragic and dramatic story that rarely happens. The striking thing is that no matter how hard the adoptive parents tried to make him belong to the family, Mandy never felt he truly belonged to them. This feeling of not belonging was probably brought about by the especially sharp contrasts between him and the children of the adoptive parents.

There are, on the other hand, many other adopted children who adjust very well to their adoptive families, especially when they feel a sense of belongingness. Somehow, it seems easier if there are no natural siblings to contend with. We will see this in the following case.

Arbie was a seven-year-old boy adopted by a doctor and his wife. They later adopted a girl, three years younger than Arbie. Figure 22 gives Arbie's genogram.

The two children were both intellectually gifted but underwent only a few group play-therapy sessions, because of some feelings of hostility they were experiencing. They both knew from the very beginning that they were adopted, and that they had been especially chosen from among many other children. They were also brought to the nuns' convent for a visit and were told that they had come from this convent. These issues were worked out in therapy through play. Both children are now reported to be doing well.

Another case involved four natural siblings. The adopted girl, Myrna, seemed to have adjusted only after there occurred a lot of testing the limits, questioning, and searching for her real mother. Myrna's genogram is shown in figure 23.

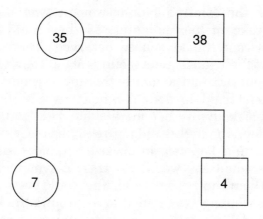

Figure 22. Arbie's Genogram

The adoptive father was a successful businessman while the mother was a well-known designer. Although her two elder sisters were very much taller, Myrna had the prettiest face of all. She was adopted when she was two years old. Her mother

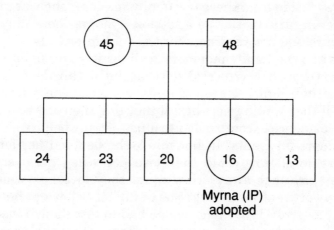

Figure 23. Myrna's Genogram

used to be the family's laundrywoman who requested the family to take in her daughter, as they could provide her with the decent life Myrna so deserved. They granted her request, but their subsequent feelings about the adoption had to be worked out during the family therapy sessions.

Myrna started to act-out when she was fourteen. She continually asked why her mother left her, and she claimed that her adoptive parents did not really love her. She was also negativistic and belligerent toward her older sisters. There were times when she would get their earrings or wear their blouses without their permission. She would even lend those to her friends who always seemed to be around the house. Once, when scolded for coming home late and not even bothering to call her parents about her whereabouts, she ran away and slept in a friend's house. She also cut classes and got into trouble in school.

During the family sessions, her feelings toward her parents and siblings were worked through, as well as their feelings toward her. Although the parents, especially the father, constantly reassured her, they also made it known that there were limits to her behavior. They pointed out that her misbehavior would have corresponding punishment and negative consequences. Aside from these few family sessions, she was made to face her natural mother in a session. This was done only when she expressed her readiness for the encounter.

When the family members' feelings were brought out and worked through, Myrna realized that she had all along just been testing their limits. Unconsciously , she had been acting badly to see if they would reject her. If they did, then she would have ample evidence to confirm her feelings of truly being unloved by her adoptive parents. In her mind, she doubted her adoptive parents' love. How could they love her when her very own mother gave her away? How could they love her when she was unworthy of their love? She could not believe in her heart that they truly loved her, so she had to test them. When they did not reject her, she then began to believe that she was indeed worthy of their love and that they genuinely cared for her in spite of her misbehavior.

It was equally important for Myrna to realize that there were limits and consequences to her behavior, which her parents were ready to impose consistently. Besides, it was also a relief for her to hear directly from her natural mother why she was given away to the family which could take care of her. Her natural mother loved her so much she did not want to make her suffer. Thus, the roots of her identity were worked out, and she began to appreciate her adoptive parents.

Brenda was the only child of an elderly couple who sent her to the best schools and provided her with all possible support. She was the natural daughter of a woman who died at childbirth. The father could no longer provide adequately for his eight children, so he requested the adoptive couple who personally knew the natural mother to take in Brenda, and they gladly accepted. Because they were not aware of the repercussions of not telling Brenda she was adopted, they never bothered to tell her of her adoption.

Although things were not all that smooth, the family was able to handle Brenda's outbursts reasonably well. There did not seem to be any major problems until "all hell broke loose." One day, Brenda, who was already nineteen, was looking through some papers in her mother's drawers when she saw her adoption papers. She was dumbfounded. She became very hysterical and violent toward her parents who, she felt, betrayed her. Unable to control herself, Brenda slashed her wrists (not too deeply) and demanded to see her natural parents. She was then told of the circumstances of her adoption. Brenda demanded to see her natural father, whom the adoptive parents located. Father and daughter were brought together, and Brenda has clung to him desperately even to the point of asking that her name be legally changed to his, so that she could use her "real name." This was done immediately.

Brenda underwent intensive therapy with joint treatment provided by a psychologist and a psychiatrist. Needless to say, the core issues in her therapy revolved around her identity and lack of self-worth. She indulged in a lot of testing behavior and was extremely ambivalent toward her adoptive parents who remained steady and firm.

With consistent monitoring, she was able to finish a two-year secretarial course. She also had a boyfriend who helped increase her self-esteem, but she had to part from him because he was already married and had a family of his own. The parting brought about another crisis in her life which interrupted her healing. After being helped to work through her feelings of rejection, she eventually recovered but is still under the guidance of her psychiatrist.

From the cases mentioned and others not detailed here, it seems that certain common patterns are observable among adoptive families. From the adopted child's viewpoint, some observations stand out.

First. The child always feels a need to question his or her identity. Questions like these always arise: Why did my parents give me away? Why did they leave me? Did they not love me? Was I not worthy of their love? How could my adoptive parents love me when my real parents have given me away?

Second. The child experiences a need to test his or her adoptive parents' love by doing things that would normally make the parents reject him or her. This is done in order to confirm whether or not he or she is worthy of their love. This is usually done unconsciously.

Third. The child feels a need to find his or her natural parents. The adoptive child needs to trace back, find the roots and attain his or her real identity once and for all.

On the part of the adoptive parents, some guidelines are helpful.

First. It is better for the child to know directly from them, and not from other sources, of his or her adoption. This must be made known to the child as soon as his or her cue questions reveal his or her readiness.

Second. There is a need not to get hooked to the testing and rejection game. Parents need to be steady and reassuring because the child's testing behavior is related to his or her own self-worth, not some parents' fault.

Third. While being steady and reassuring, parents need to set limits and concrete consequences, or punishment for any wrongdoing. They must not be afraid to implement consequences agreed upon, despite the child's maneuverings.

Fourth and last. The whole family must be involved in dealing with their own feelings toward the child as well as his or her own reactions to them. The most crucial aspect in therapy here is that the child must obtain a real sense of belonging in the adoptive family.

Further Discussion

The cases presented in this chapter point to the fact that living with a special child, whether autistic, gifted, retarded, or adopted, requires some special adjustments from family members. They further tell us that these special children do have needs they genuinely feel, and these the parents and siblings must meet. It is all-important to discern what these real needs are and to distinguish them from simple capriciousness arising from a lack of attention. Setting limits is also necessary, so that the child's capriciousness does not lead to self-centeredness.

In dealing with their special children, parents are well-reminded to make use of the ***total person approach,*** i.e., to consider the child's intellectual, emotional, social, moral, and physical needs. This total approach should be their continuing guide and framework for parenting.

The tremendous implications of this total-person framework cannot be overemphasized since it extends beyond the family — to the nation as a whole.

When, for example, gifted children are not guided constructively, when they are not imbued with proper moral values, when their physical, social, and emotional needs are not fulfilled, they tend to look for stimulating outlets that usually turn out to be destructive. That is why we see bright street children who are clever at stealing and lying, at picking locks and pockets. They turn out to be manipulative juvenile deliquents constantly outsmarting law-enforcing authorities.

The most striking and unforgettable example of a gifted person with a lopsided personal development is still that of the brilliant intellectual giant who became a ruthless dictator and ruled the Philippines for twenty years, plundering, stealing, and lying to an entire nation. He was intellectually gifted but his moral development was stunted and even distorted. This is one memorable case where the intellect was nurtured to the neglect of the person's moral facet.

As the child moves along different stages of development, parents and other child caretakers would do well to refer to the total-person framework and become constantly aware, every step of the way, of whatever aspect in the child's growth is lagging behind. They can then shift focus and start to pay attention to that particular aspect.

One simple and concrete exercise that I have found helpful is to ask parents to write down ten or more words or phrases to describe a particular child or person. I let them do this very quickly so that no editing or only minimum censoring is done. I then ask the parents to examine the list, counting how many words pertain to the child's intellectual aspects, how many to the emotional aspect, the social, moral, and physical. Immediately after this examination, the parents easily notice the areas of attention and neglect in their parenting. The parents can then make a conscious effort to focus on particular aspects by providing specific activities and asking the relevant quetions that lead their child to value those sides of his or her person.

7

The Not-So-Special Child

HOW A FAMILY AS A SYSTEM coped with having a special child was the subject of chapter 6. On the other side of the coin, how is an average child to cope with a family of intellectually gifted individuals? In other words, what problems does the not-so-special child meet in a special or exceptional family? Often, such a child, who has no readily identifiable outstanding characteristics, becomes different in a negative way. In the family context, how does this child attempt to find his place? He is, in a lot of families, the Identified Patient (IP). This child is usually referred to the clinical psychologist for "slowness in understanding lessons" and for "lack of motivation" in school.

"Where Do I Fit In?"

In an article, "The Filipino Child and His Family" (1979), I described briefly the case of Marie, a lively twelve-year-old girl who was the youngest in a family of four children. She had two sisters and a brother. She was referred to me by her parents because she was "rebellious, insecure, and incurably lazy."

They said they could not trust her with any responsibility. While her elder sisters were excelling in academics as well as in such extracurricular activities as swimming, Marie seemed not to be trying at all. "She cannot seem to follow any of the rules we set up," her parents concluded. The parents were also at a loss in trying to find one thing Marie could do better than her prettier and smarter elder sisters.

Marie revealed, "I used to try hard to do what my parents wanted but nothing I do seems to please them. Even if my sisters do not exert any effort, they still get my parents' love and attention. Even my *lola* seems to like them more. Now I am getting all the attention because they are concerned about my attitude and, of course, because I am coming here to see you. But it is useless to try to be good. I guess it is because my eldest sister is a scholar and the one next to her is very pretty and good in everything." What was clearly unsaid — the necessary corollary to her statements, or so it seemed to me, were these questions: "Where do I fit in? What is my place in my family? How can I have a position and value of my own?"

Apart from the obvious favoritism, people often dismiss rebelliousness of this kind as "attention-getting behavior." This label merely describes the behavior; it does not, however, explain what is really going on underneath. What then is the message underlying this attention-getting behavior?

At this stage in her development, Marie was beginning to search for an identity uniquely hers. Her need to feel a sense of competence had not been adequately fulfilled, and yet she was already entering adolescence.

It was only after a few family-counseling sessions that Marie finally "found her place" and felt recognized for her being full of fun, caring, and even-tempered. The presence of the *lolo* who seemed to understand her helped a lot in the process. The *lolo* was an artist, and he discovered Marie's talent in drawing and handicraft. The family also "discovered" her good sense of humor and affectionate nature. They became aware that, when given a clear and specific area of responsibility, Marie could be reasonably responsible. Thus, she was no longer expected to be like her elder sisters in everything; she now felt valued for what she really was — a different but equally worthy person.

Consequently, she achieved more in school because her motivation and self-confidence had greatly increased.

Pura, a frail-looking nine-year-old girl, was brought in by her parents because she was "lazy in her studies, and she never finishes her final exams." Her parents explained that she would do reasonably well in the quizzes but when it came to the final exams, she would block out. Pura was also described as quite playful. But "she can do much better," according to her father.

Pura was the youngest in a family of four children, as shown in her genogram (figure 24).

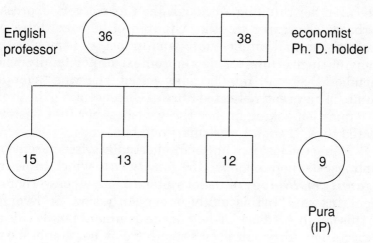

Figure 24. Pura's Genogram

Her mother was thirty-six years old, a professor of English in a big Manila university. She had written two books and was a very active leader in the academe. Her father was an economist and a Ph.D. holder. Her fifteen-year-old *ate* was a gold medalist in school, and her two brothers were both in the top ten of their class.

When interviewed, the two older brothers both found her to be quite slow and said they merely tolerated Pura's remarks during dinner time for the reason that she was corny and dumb. They said they were not "that shallow"when they were her age.

On the other hand, her *ate* said that Pura was just immature because she had been babied. She found her cute and entertaining at times.

Because of the nature of the complaint, Pura was subsequently interviewed and was given several psychological tests, including a comprehensive Intelligence Quotient (IQ) profile and some projective tests.

Results revealed a high average IQ with no subtest score that was below the average range. This indicated that Pura was not "dumb." Even in her interview, she was alert and logical in her thinking, although she was not very expressive verbally. Compared to other children of her age, Pura was perfectly normal intellectually and in fact was smarter than some of them. However, in the context of her family whose members were all intellectually gifted, she was "slow and dumb." This greatly affected Pura's self-concept. To the projective question asking for her three wishes, her first wish was stated thus, "I wish I was smart and big."

Being the last in a line of intellectually gifted parents and siblings, she had to follow the *family rule* which came from a *family mythology* or belief system. That, when verbalized, went this way: "In this family, no one can be slow" or "Everyone in this family is smart." This was the dominant family rule and expectation. Although she was neither slow nor dumb, she was not as gifted as her siblings; so she was different. Hence, she did not rightfully belong and was clearly the IP.

Her blocking out during exams seemed to have been brought about by a strong pressure upon her — to be an achiever in school. The more nervous and anxious she became, the more she forgot. It could also be an unconscious need to rebel against the family myth and a way of asserting herself. It was as if she was saying, "Take me and love me as I am, even if I am different from you."

When the genogram and the total picture of the family was explained to Pura's parents and siblings in a feedback session, they could not grasp it at first. The family mythology and resulting expectations were very deeply ingrained in both

their conscious and unconscious minds. It was just unthinkable! Other achievement areas were explored, areas where
Pura could excel. They finally agreed to help her discover her
artistic talents since she loved to draw and paint. After a while,
they also started to really listen to her and see things from her
point of view. It took more than a year before they were able to
be genuinely proud of her and her artwork.

Another "not-so-special" child was Larry, a fourteen-year-
old adolescent of average intelligence in a family of achievers.
He was brought in to me by his father because of his "below
average academic performance."

His genogram (figure 25) is self-explanatory:

Even though the family could well afford to send Larry,
like the rest of his siblings, to exclusive schools, he could not
gain acceptance owing to his low entrance and achievement
scores.

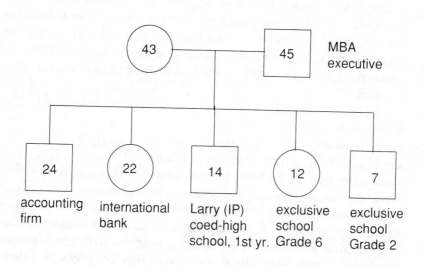

Figure 25. Larry's Genogram

His father was a top-level executive in one of the country's biggest accounting firms, where Larry's eldest brother also worked. On the other hand, his elder sister had a good job in an international bank. Larry's younger brother and sister were enrolled in exclusive private schools which were well known for their high academic standards. His mother was a college graduate of a business course who had opted to become a full-time housewife. She was perceived to be quite strict with Larry. Being the middle sibling in a family of achievers whose intellectual gifts he did not share, Larry was vulnerable, and he turned out to be the passive and shy IP. He was notably lacking in initiative and self-confidence.

The last illustrative example (Danny's case) gives us a picture of how the extended family plays a big role in the upbringing of the average child in an achieving family.

Danny was a five-year-old kindergarten pupil in a private preschool. His father was a Commerce graduate, working in an average-sized business firm. His mother was a preschool teacher.

Danny was referred to me for evaluation "because he had started to become difficult to handle." He wanted to be fed by his mother and to sleep with his parents every night. He also became disobedient and was observed to be daydreaming in school. His family lived in a compound where his *lolo* and *lola* (paternal grandparents), as well as his aunts and uncles, also resided.

The "big family," of which the illustrious *lolo* was the head, was made up of two young families whose fathers were both his sons. The "big family" was very closely knit and the grandparents, aunts and uncles were all very caring and nurturing adults. In fact, Danny would play with his cousins who were about his age every day. The *lolo* was a very prominent economist who held a top government position. He was known for being a brilliant, honest, and hardworking public servant and philanthropist. Danny was the first grandson in this renowned family. His genogram (figure 26) gives us a clear picture of the family constellation.

The twenty-eight-year-old uncle was said to be brilliant and was following in the footsteps of his much-admired father. His children all seemed to be precocious: After playing with

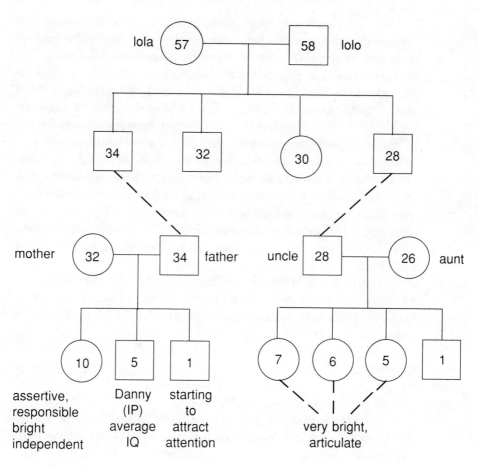

Figure 26. Danny's Genogram

them, Danny would usually come home with questions, wondering why his cousins did things differently in their home.

Danny's parents were very hardworking. Both held full-time jobs and still managed to run a bakeshop near their home. In his projective drawings, Danny perceived his parents as "always working." In fact, Danny was so concerned for his family that he would always ask his parents, "Are we family?"

In his Draw-a-Person Test, he referred to the male and female drawings as his younger brother and sister; he had no drawing of himself. In the family drawings, however, he merely drew his parents and himself to form the complete picture of his family — as if wishing that he be the only child in the family. In his fantasy, Larry was the only significant child. This also revealed his preoccupation with or perception of his younger brother and sister as key rivals for his parents' attention. Aside from this, being the first male *apo* (grandchild) in this prominent family of achievers, he sensed he not only had to find his place, but also had to live up to a lot of inevitable expectations. How then does a boy (the first *apo*) of average intelligence — surrounded by bright and articulate siblings and cousins in a renowned family of achievers — find his place?

The cases of Marie, Pura, Larry, and Danny are only four examples of a common phenomenon which brings the special family to seek help regarding the average child who sometimes stands out as the Identified Patient.

Further Discussion

Family mythology refers to the beliefs which the family adheres to, which become part of their self-concept or self-definition. A self-definition, for example, is enunciated this way: "No Aquino ever gets low grades in school." The family member who acts and behaves to destroy this myth is most likely to become the **IP**. The strength or force of this mythology comes from the fact that it is usually unconscious. The rules and expectations that come from this belief are usually unarticulated.

In my talks with parents, the first thing I ask them to do is to ask themselves some basic questions about their families. These may be: What are your expectations of your children? What do you value most about your child? About your family? What kinds of questions do you ask them? What messages are you consciously or unconsciously sending?

For one family, we examined in detail the questions the parents usually asked their children. They came up with such questions as, "How was your test?"; "Did you do your home-work?"; and "How are your grades?" Very seldom did it occur that the questions were "Did you help your friend today?" or "How's P.E.?"

Although nothing seems to be wrong with the "academi-cally inclined" questions, they send this kind of message to the children: The most important, if not the only important thing, is that children must perform well academically.

Asking questions is one of the most powerful ways of imparting a message. They subtly tell what the important things are. The children eventually can pick up their message very quickly because they need to gain their parents' recognition and approval. The questions tell the children the things their parents value.

One basic guideline for families so they can cope with this problem is the use of the ***total person developmental framework*** for a well-rounded personality. (This framework also applies to gifted children as we have seen earlier.) In monitoring the child or adolescent's development, parents may constantly check if they are giving value to the child's emotional, social, physical, moral, and intellectual sides. This helps guard against the fostering of a lopsided development that breeds intellectual geniuses who are emotionally retarded, and morally and socially inept.

In helping the child find his or her place in the family, as well as in the world, a healthy self-concept with a sense of competence is essential. Using the multidimensional framework like the Rubik's Cube (Carandang 1981), we can see that there are many doors to the self. The child may excel in music, in the arts, in dancing: his or her mechanical aptitude may be very high, too. Although these aptitudes may be common knowledge, in the family it is not enough that they remain mere knowledge. Parents must genuinely value these nonacademic talents and communicate their importance to the child. Saying, for example, "Sa arts na lang siya" ("She'll just be in the arts") is not giving value to a child's artistic talents. Furthermore, the siblings can be taught to value these nonacademic areas only if the parents set the example. From there, the siblings can start to regard their other brother or sister from a new perspective. They can be understanding without being condescending.

A cornerstone, or building block, for a healthy self-concept is a sense of competence. The child who faces the world with "I can" rather than "I can't" is way ahead in his or her development. This sense of competence can start in any area, such as biking, running, playing the guitar, and the like (Carandang 1979). The important thing is not the content but the feeling the child gets by knowing he or she is good at something, no matter what it is. This way of building up the child's self-worth can then be the starting point at which the average child can find his or her own place and value in the exceptional family. When self-worth is not established, a negative self-concept is developed, and this can have frightening consequences later on.

8

Suicides and Siblings of Suicides

FEELINGS OF WORTHLESSNESS, feelings of isolation, and pressure to achieve are the most commonly cited causes of suicide.

In Metro Manila, the past five years have seen the rise of suicides among our young people. The media have given considerable attention to the suicide of movie starlets and college students. Not as widely publicized were the suicides among intelligent adolescents and young adults studying in exclusive schools and who were from well-to-do families, who seemed to be reacting to extreme pressures to achieve in school.

It would seem that with intimate family relationships and supportive extended families among Filipinos, feelings of isolation, loneliness and lack of self-worth are not much of a problem. However, there has been a noticeable increase in the cases of attempted suicides and siblings of completed suicides that have been referred to my clinic.

Why do young people get to the point of actual self-annihilation? This question becomes more significant when one considers the existence in the country of strong religious and predominantly Christian orientation and close family ties.

There seems to be a need for systematic research focusing on cultural factors related to the problem.

In this chapter, the family dynamics involving two generations of suicides in a large extended family are explored in detail. The case has been selected because of its rich and complex dynamics. It also illustrates how a great number of insights and key concepts in family therapy can be abstracted from a single case.

Presentation of the case is followed by two brief accounts of the suicides' siblings who have come for psychological help. Although much has been written on the phenomenon of suicide, very little exploration has been done about its impact on the suicide's siblings and other family members.

Two Generations of Suicides

The center of the extended family under study rested on the old couple — X and Y. X was seventy-two, while Y was seventy-three. In order not to complicate the overall diagram unnecessarily, only the sketches of the families directly involved were drawn. All the couple's children were married and had their own families. Except the deceased and the youngest (G), who had lived out of the country with his own family, the rest of the family members lived in the same compound which was the original home of the parents, X and Y. The genogram of the extended family and living unit concerned is given in figure 27.

Although the family experienced several crises in the past, the family asked for psychiatric help for the first time when E, the fifth sibling, then in his early twenties, was found in the bathroom covered with blood after slashing his wrist. That was the first clear signal that the family was in trouble. E went into therapy, seemed to recover, but underwent no follow-up treatment. Furthermore, because E was seen as the only patient, family relationships were not explored. E was simply labeled as manic- depressive and regarded as the sick one in the family.

Since his suicide attempt, E had been in and out of the hospital and had been seeing different psychiatrists. He even receive several electroconvulsive treatments. He would get his

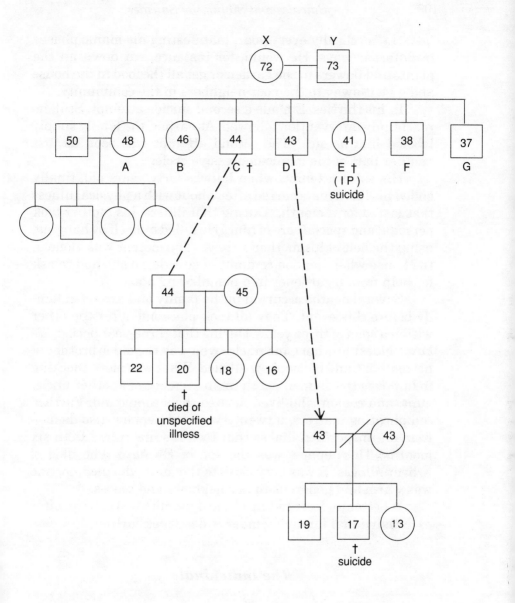

Figure 27. Genogram of the Family
of Two Suicides

"attacks" cyclically every year, manifesting his manic phases in different ways. He would, for instance, cut down all the plants and flowers in the garden or get all the food in the house and give it away to the poor neighbors in the community.

In his thirties, E made a second suicide attempt. Still, no real family intervention followed. As earlier, the family simply labeled him as sick. The second attempt was seen as just another part of his manic-depressive cycle.

His third attempt, when he was forty years old, finally ended his life. This occurred after a bout with a physical illness that lasted for a month. (During that illness, his mother took personal and special care of him.) He killed himself by hanging, using the belt of his mother's dress. The mother was alone in the house when her son committed suicide, so she had to ask for help from a gardener in a neighboring house.

Several deaths occurred in the family and extended family before this event. They all took place one after the other within a span of three years. During that three-year period, E's *kuya* (eldest brother), his uncle (who was the older brother of his mother), and his nephew all died. What was more shocking to him was the sudden death in an accident of another uncle, aunt, and cousin who lived next to their compound. Further complicating matters, a twenty-year-old nephew also died — from an unspecified illness that took his life in less than six months. This nephew was the son of E's *kuya* who died of a liver illness. E was very close to the aunt who died, for she was warm and generous to her nephews and nieces.

A better understanding of the dynamics will emerge after each individual family member is described further.

The Individuals

X, seventy-two years old, was an intellectually brilliant matriarch who was the eldest in her own family. She had an older brother, a brilliant economist, who had a large family of his own. X was undoubtedly her father's favorite. Her father was a self-sacrificing, upright, and prominent but humble government official. He was a journalist who fought graft and corruption fearlessly. X closely identified with her father, who in turn recognized her brilliance. He seemed to communicate even better with her than with his own wife, who was more of a diligent and conscientious housewife.

Although the *ate* in the family, X was exempted from a lot of household chores, since she was made to excel in piano and the fine arts. She was given special praise for her musical gifts and her writing abilities. She was one of the first women to drive a car in the community. While she spent her time developing her fine talents, her only sister who was very much younger than she became the *tagasaló* (see chapter 5) who was expected to do household chores and the like.

Y, seventy-three years old, was a successful lawyer who became the dean of a law college. He was small in build, very quiet and reserved. He was described by his wife as an indifferent husband and father, for he was involved in neither childrearing nor household matters. The house was almost entirely the domain of his wife, X, who complained about Y's lack of concern for the needs of his growing children.

A, forty-eight years old, held a master's degree in business administration and had a good job. She had to support her five children and grandchildren because her husband had died two years ago. He had had a congenital renal problem, making him difficult to live with, even during the early part of the marriage. A also took care of her chronically ill mother-in-law. For the past five years, she and her family had lived in another town, but recently she had moved with her family back to the original compound.

B, forty-six years old, was a cancer specialist who held a very high position in a hospital. She also had a clinic near her home and was usually called upon by relatives for medical help. She married a college dropout who owned a garment store that went bankrupt about ten years after their marriage. During the first ten or fifteen years of her marriage, her husband was very demanding and would insist on having sexual intimacies even when she had been exhausted by overnight duty as a medical resident. In one of their quarrels, he poked a gun at her temple when she did not give in to his overtures. Because of these difficulties and a financial setback, she moved to her parents' compound along with her five children. Of the five children, four were girls who all achieved considerable success in their respective schools and careers. The eldest daughter became a doctor who got married and had three children. This daughter and her own family lived in a small house adjacent to B's (her mother's house) in the original compound, but they took their meals at B's home. B's remaining children were either working or finishing their college courses — except the only boy (the fourth in the family), who became a high school dropout.

C, forty-four years old, was a very bright man who finished law school. However, he never completed his bar exams to enable him to practice law independently. He married a townmate with whom he had four children. After marriage, he built a house adjacent to his parents'. He was known to be a very honest civic worker in the community. His mother (X) felt his death (from a liver illness) to be a very great loss, because he was very attentive and supportive of her. He was E's *kuya*, whose son died of an unspecified illness less than six months from the time of diagnosis — one in the series of deaths that took place in the crucial three-year period.

D, forty-three years old, was the only sibling who did not finish college. Although he looked very much like his father, he was not close to him. Neither was he close to his mother (unlike C and E who were both close to her). Though he was very bright and creative, D saw himself as the middle sibling left out of the family. Even when he was past forty, he still remained bitter as he was greatly convinced that he was an outsider. When he was younger, D would cling to the pet dogs and would even sleep with them. This was probably how he tried to have his nurturing needs met. If not with his pets, he was always in the company of peers, cousins, and neighbors — all to whom he felt very close. He became a pilot, and he married a next-door neighbor whose brothers were his *barkada* (peer group). His wife finished high school with much difficulty for she was not very intelligent. After ten years, he separated from her. This was the only marital separation in the family. D's ten years of marriage produced three sons. The mother took the eldest one upon the separation. The youngest one stayed with B, the cancer specialist aunt, who raised him, together with her own five children, in the original compound. He got along well with his cousins and, with them, studied in the same private school.

The middle son, on the other hand, was left in the custody of the father, who was insecure at that time, owing to his job problems.

At seventeen, this middle son of B committed suicide by hanging himself after a quarrel with his girlfriend. History seemed to repeat itself: He became the second-generation suicide, in the exact manner of his uncle E. Like his father, the middle sibling felt left out and adrift, finding his needed feeling of connection only in his girlfriend. But when she broke off with him, all connections were gone. Being a very intense adolescent, he ended his life a year after his uncle committed suicide — as if taking after him.

E, forty-one years old, the IP of the family, was a lawyer who managed to pass the bar exams even though he was hospitalized on and off just before taking them. He was the obvious IP for about twenty years: He tried to commit suicide in his twenties, then in his thirties, and finally completed the act in his forties. E was a very bright and sensitive boy who was also very sickly and anemic. Although he was frequently absent from school, he managed to remain at the top of his class. He was particularly good in English, mathematics and geometry. He was, however, extremely shy and unassertive in school.

For a long time, he had been acting out his need for help from the family in ways that would be dismissed as merely *sumpong* (occasional behavioral outbursts). Aside from slashing his wrists and neck, he would also disappear at times only to be found later in the neighborhood, helping the poor people. He would cut down all the plants and flowers in the garden, then turn depressive for days.

While still a preadolescent, he witnessed the hysterics of his otherwise strong and dominant mother who learned that her quiet and passive husband had a mistress. His mother's hysterical outbursts were repeated several times in the night. Being an alert and sensitive child, he remembered being terrified by the outbursts. Eventually, he became very empathic toward his mother and increasingly resentful toward his father. The vivid quarrels and cold war between his parents troubled him so much that he was observed to daydream frequently in school. He also became quite absent-minded. All these were simply dismissed as signs of shyness.

Although introverted, he had a girlfriend in high school whom he adored. She was a bright, attractive, and assertive young woman. Their relationship continued after high school, but in college they parted ways when the girl felt she had outgrown him. Their separation left E despondent. It was also during this time that his mother unwittingly poured out her heartaches to him, because the father never outgrew his fondness for mistresses. This made him harbor deeper resentments toward his father and develop a protective and symbiotic relationship with his mother. In turn, she became protective of him because he was very sickly. Consequently, there formed the proverbial triangle — mother, father, and son. The mother had become very bitter toward her husband and showered her love and affection on her son who reciprocated in turn. E became his mother's *tagasaló* to the extent that he married much later than the rest of his siblings.

On the other hand, the overpowered husband retaliated through his continuous "conquests" of other women who idolized him and gave him the much-needed affection and ego-boosting.

E then married a townmate who came from a family of a much lower socioeconomic status than his own. She was also not very intelligent. Predictably, E's mother and wife did not get along. His mother attributed many of his subsequent breakdowns to his wife's inability to reach his level and really understand him.

E and his wife had three children — two boys and a girl. The boy got emotional support from his cousins who, among themselves, formed a support system for the whole extended family in the compound. In this big extended family, the cousins, who were the grandchildren of X and Y, formed their own supportive group very much like a huge sibling subsystem.

F, thirty-eight years old, who had a master's degree in economics, was an extremely intelligent woman. She married a childhood sweetheart who did not finish college. She eventually became the caretaker of her husband's family business when her parents-in-law died. Her husband got into a near-fatal car accident, which required neurological medication. He was a bit younger than F and was characterized as unreliable and erratic. The couple had five children who functioned very well, as they became part of the cousins' supportive system. F had thought of leaving her husband to go abroad on her own, but the difficulty of bringing along the children prevented her from doing so. Hence, she taught business courses in a university. Her relationship with her parents (X and Y) was marked by a relative distance from her mother and an apparent closeness to her father. As a child, she was "papa's girl," being the youngest among the girls.

G, thirty-seven years old, the youngest and the only independent and successful male in the family, lived abroad with his wife and three children. He was the only one who married someone who did not reside in the same town. Being the youngest, he seemed to have been buffered from the effects of the bitter and discordant marital relationship of his parents. This is so because he left immediately after school and got a job out of the country. He held a top executive position in an international company. His wife came from a well-to-do family in an exclusive Manila suburban community. They have lived out of the country since their marriage. G would come home only for occasional visits.

The Dynamics

Let us now synthesize some significant data from the extended family dynamics so that some identifiable patterns may emerge.

First. The center, or pivotal point, of the entire family system, the marital relationship of X and Y, was characterized by bitterness and pain. This pained marital relationship affected the marriages and careers of the next generation (i.e., A, B, C, D, E, F). It seemed that the bitterness seeped through every aspect of their lives. While the matriarch was never able to forgive her husband for his infidelities or to let go of the marriage relationship, the patriarch made no real attempts to change his behavior. He remained passive-aggressive in response to his wife's dominance. The couple never attempted to obtain therapeutic intervention through marital therapy.

Second. Following the identification and modeling principles, all the females (A, B, and F) turned out to be strong and successful in their careers. However, they all married nonachievers who had to be taken care of. Following a pattern, not one of the females separated from her husband in spite of unsatisfactory marital relationships.

Third. All the males, except the youngest (G, the one who got away from the system) were underachievers. Of the rest, only the IP (or E) who subsequently committed suicide completed a degree which allowed him to practice law independently. Just the same, he was not able to live independently from his parents because of his illness and his symbiotic relationship with his mother.

Fourth. Except for the youngest child, all of the children got married to spouses who lived either in the neighborhood or within the community. Not one of their own families lived far away from home. In fact, almost all of them ended up living together in an old compound. From the outsider's viewpoint, they seemed to be a closely knit family. Nonexistent, however, was the warmth and intimacy in the relationships.

Fifth. The matriarch (X) was the power in the family (cf. the next chapter on power). She was the critic, judge, and decision-maker — the source of ultimate judgment on how good or bad each one in the family was. She was usually negative, critical, and bitter toward her husband and children, and the next generation absorbed this attitude and unconsciously brought it into their own marriages. Furthermore, the bitterness she felt because of her husband's philandering, the "wrath of the woman scorned," permeated all the lives of the entire family.

Although the power was obviously in the hands of the dominant and strong matriarch, the shy husband (Y) retaliated or wielded his own power through his philandering: "I'll hit you where it hurts the most." He never gave up his deadly weapon. He, of course, unconsciously made sure his wife knew about his mistresses.

Moreover, the patriarch had another source of power — being the breadwinner. His wife did not work outside the home after marriage, so she was dependent on him for all the household needs. He did not make life easy for her. The husband himself also had a dominant mother who made him use her maiden name when she discovered her husband had other women. Although his own mother was his source of nurture, Y had a great need to show his own power or perhaps follow the footsteps of his late father whose name he could not use. Interestingly though, his elder brother used their father's name.

Although slight of build, shy and introverted, Y found his own source of power in being attractive to women, as well as in his capability to earn money. Uncanny, though, was the fact that in the last three years of his life, he suffered as if symbolically from cancer of the prostate glands, which caused him intense pain. Even then, it was his wife who bathed, nursed, and took care of him all throughout his illness.

Sixth. The grandchildren, numbering around twenty, formed their own support system. They drew their strength from one another and from outsiders, such as their aunts, uncles, friends, and teachers. It is encouraging to see how the third generation can still surface with their own strength, and form something like a sibling subsystem. When one of them died (D's seventeen-year-old son who committed suicide), the grandchildren banded together and openly shared their feelings with one another.

Seventh. The old couple never discussed their feelings openly or tried to seek professional help, except during the IP's suicide attempts. Even then, they undertook no follow-ups. The heavy and bitter air in the family was never cleared. Everyone just breathed in this poisonous air day in and day out. They stayed with one another for a semblance of togetherness, of the need for companionship and emotional security. The same dynamics operated in the marital unions of the next generation — the old couple's children. Somehow, a magnet drew them close together: The high standards the matriarch set as a judge and critic seemed to draw them all back to the old home. This attraction to the old home may also reflect the children's search for the much-needed recognition and approval which they never received from their parents.

In this closely knit extended family — where the air was filled with heaviness and despondency — it seemed that the suicide by hanging of the two male middle siblings (E and D's

middle son) belonging to two different but successive generations were desperate cries for help in a suffocating family
atmosphere. There seemed to be no other way out for these two.

Siblings of Suicides

In suicide cases, discussion dwells on the suicides themselves, usually not on their impact on members of the family.
The pain, shame, and guilt that the survivors have to live with
have been the subject of fiction, but not of scientific research.

It is sometimes theorized that killing one's self is the
ultimate way of unconsciously getting back at the family, especially at the parents. This implies that the suicidal act is not
just an act of despair but also a rebellious and vengeful act of
anger. One could also speculate that the impact of the suicidal
act on the Filipino family would be more intense than that in
other cultures, owing to the Filipinos' religious orientation and
close family ties.

It also seems natural to think that the impact is felt
differently by the members of the family. Following are brief
accounts of two siblings whose elder brothers committed suicide.

Reynaldo, a fifteen-year-old boy, was brought in to the
clinic for "excessive praying." His mother reported that he
would pray from six until eleven o'clock in the evening, interrupted only by dinner, which he ate hurriedly. His *kuya* had
died through suicide more than a year before the referral, so his
family never related his behavior to the suicide. It turned out
that a few days before his *kuya* killed himself, Reynaldo had a
mild argument with him. Up to the present, Reynaldo was still
trying to ward off his intense guilt through his obsessive-
compulsive praying rituals.

Reynaldo was a diligent and conscientious student who
was at the top of his class, before he became obsessed with praying. His mother was a grade school principal who valued hard
work and discipline. She herself had not resolved her own guilt
about her son's death. This guilt feeling Reynaldo absorbed,
and it added to his own guilt. Noticing Reynaldo's failing
grades, the mother became very worried that his praying

(although "good behavior") was interfering with his studies. The father was passive and helpless about the situation. I discovered that the family had not really gone through the stages of mourning for the dead son. They had not allowed this intense mixture of feelings to surface into awareness — into expressing and discussing them openly with one another.

Anton, seventeen years old, was also the sibling of a *kuya* who committed suicide. He was the middle sibling in a family of five children. Anton's grades were all failing at the time of the referral. He was also observed to be despondent and sad most of the time. He seemed to be grieving for the entire family that was left behind. Complicating matters was that, about two years prior to the suicide, the family had experienced another loss: Their mother separated from her alcoholic husband. Anton had begun to have suicidal ideations and this further alarmed the mother. Fortunately, another elder brother, twenty years old, was around to work out his depression in therapy. Consequently, this *kuya* became the therapeutic ally in the family, while being supported by the therapist. He helped a lot because Anton looked up to him as his elder brother and followed his example.

The two younger brothers in the examples cited — Reynaldo and Anton — acted out their guilt and depression in different forms. The first one tried to ward off depression and possible suicidal thoughts through obsessive-compulsive praying, while the other one allowed the depression to sink in. In both cases, it was significant for the family to first recognize and become aware that they were all going through the pain of grieving. It was equally important to use the available human resources within the family, so that the members could be strengthened as they tried to cope with the problems.

Further Discussion

In reviewing the points brought out by the preceding cases, some insights on family dynamics related to suicide are worth highlighting. The following pointers can help surviving members of the family cope with the loss and the pain.

First. Of utmost importance is the quality of the marital relationship. A pained and bitter marriage, when not confronted and resolved in some way, leads to a heavy and depressive tone that permeates the whole family atmosphere. When dealt with in family therapy, there will necessarily be a change in the relationship — there will either be forgiveness, acceptance, or a resolve to stop hurting each other. In some cases, when it is impossible to live together, a marital separation may be agreed upon. Somehow, the oppressive atmosphere must be cleared and family members ought to feel that they have options. In the case of X and Y, no acceptable option was seen because no open discussion of their marital problem took place. The couple and members of the family consequently felt trapped. Ultimately, for some, the only way out was suicide.

Second. The most vulnerable and sensitive among the family — perhaps owing to an inborn temperament, birth-order position, and other factors — feel the brunt and carry the burden. In the family of the couple X and Y, the one that carried the burden was E, the fifth sibling, who was the closest to his mother and who absorbed much of her bitterness. In the process, he tried to take care of her and the family, but he also felt trapped and helpless.

Third. When there is no awareness of the family dynamics of the suicide, the cycle usually repeats itself. Perhaps through the very powerful principle of **modeling**, the suicide of E was repeated in the same manner by the next generation (i.e., the son of D). The classic example of an ongoing cycle that is repeated from generation to generation is child abuse: The abusive mother is herself usually a victim of child abuse at the hands of her mother.

Fourth. Through modeling, the male-female identification with the parental figures happens unconsciously. In the family of X and Y, the daughters were strong, achieving, and dominant, while the males (except the youngest who went away) were all passive and dependent. The women all stayed with their husbands in spite of unsatisfying relationships, following the family mythology set by the matriarch.

Fifth. A supportive sibling subsystem can emerge only after some perspective is achieved — so it usually emerges in the third generation. It may be the result of opportunities for the younger generation to discuss and express feelings openly with one another and with supportive nonfamily members.

This illustrative case of the subsystem operating in the extended family of X and Y again emphasizes the need to look at the total family dynamics and context in helping suicidal children, adolescents, and adults.

The whole family should be helped to go through the grieving and mourning process together. Denial, although a usual first step, must not be allowed too long. The obsessive-compulsive praying of Reynaldo surfaced because the parents had not allowed themselves to feel the pain, the guilt, and the loss of their elder son; hence, they did not progress into the different stages of grieving. The younger son seemed to be mourning for everyone, but he too did not allow himself to feel the pain. Instead, he warded it off through his ritualistic behavior.

Members of the family have to go through the mourning process together, although they may be progressing at different stages of mourning: some may be at the anger stage, while others are still at the denial stage. They should respect one another's individual pace, but it is important that they realize they must feel that they are together and can turn to one another for support.

9

The Power in the Family

THE CONCEPT OF POWER, together with three other dimensions, was formulated by French (1977) in a fourfold table which is used to assess the configuration of family functioning. The four-dimensional table is shown below.

Four Dimensions	High	Middle	Low
1. Degree of Anxiety			
2. Power			
3. Symptom Carrier			
4. Capacity to Change			

The four dimensions were not operationalized by French, and this conceptual framework still has to be tested and applied. I will give only a brief description of each dimension, but will focus on the dimension of power in this chapter.

The Four Dimensions

Assessing the ***degree of anxiety*** is done for each member of the family. This holds true for all the other dimensions, which are then integrated and combined to get a picture of how the entire family system works. Because this has been tested empirically, the assessment is based largely on my own clinical impressions as to how anxious a person is—as evidenced by such indicators as rapid verbalization, stiffness of the body, heavy breathing and sweating, and panicky behavior.

Power refers to the amount and kind of decisions a person is allowed to make. It may also describe how each person calls the shots — as evidenced by how the other family members follow his or her decisions, instructions, or suggestions. In short, does he or she get what he or she wants in the family? Are his or her instructions complied with by other members of the family? Does he or she have control over the others?

The ***symptom carrier*** is the one who carries the stress. He or she usually ends up as the Identified Patient (IP). This makes the therapist focus on the manifested symptoms of stress and dysfunction, such as psychosomatic illnesses, maladaptive and acting-out behavior, attention-seeking, failing grades, etc.

Capacity to change is based mostly on the therapist's clinical assessment of the person's rigidity or flexibility, openness to changes in the family, and the like.

At this point, the table may be used by the therapist as a guide to help assess the functioning of the whole family. An example of a "difficult" case in terms of the configuration is one where a child is high on the symptom-carrier role (by acting out in various ways like stealing, lying) while the mother has a very high degree of anxiety. However, the father who is high in power is low in anxiety and capacity to change. This implies that the mother sees the problem as the child is acting out; but the father who holds the power refuses to see it in the same way, thus making the mother even more anxious. She may try to seek help secretly and this may prove troublesome for the therapist. Another possible consequence is for the child to act out even more, until his behavior can no longer be ignored by the father. Eventually, the father's anxiety will increase and he may agree to come for family therapy.

Nuances of Power

In my experience, the most salient and interesting of the four dimensions is that of power. The concept of power alone requires many qualifications. When trying to figure out who has the power in the Filipino family, one almost always includes the extended family. If the therapist does not figure out the person who holds the power, he or she can be treating the IP with no changes resulting because the power-holder — who may not believe in the therapy — can sabotage the whole process. This is especially true if the IP is a child.

Deciding who holds the power, however, is not very simple and easy. It can in fact be very tricky. One rule is to find out who makes the big decisions, such as moving house, where the children will go for schooling, and the like. In my experience of looking into the dimensions of power, I have come across some patterns of recurring characteristics, which I will identify and illustrate in the following cases.

The Dominant Lola

This is perhaps the easiest to identify as seen in the following case.

Lito was an eighteen-year-old college student who dropped out of school, and who, his mother suspected, was into drugs. He was referred to me after his car crashed into a post and, as a result he was grounded for a month. Two years prior to the referral, Lito's parents had separated upon the suggestion of the *lola*. The father, now living in a house across the street since the separation, came from a less-endowed family and was not as highly educated as his wife. He could not support his family, for he was also too weak to hold a good job consistently. Worse, he even had a drinking problem. The father's situation eventually led to the separation. Since then, Lito and his mother have lived with his *lola* and other uncles.

When recounting his experiences in answer to questions, Lito always referred to his *lola*. It seemed like his parents did not play a significant role in his life. He referred to his maternal uncles, too.

The *lola* was a well-known doctor — a pioneer and leader in her field. She was respected and looked up to by younger doctors. She was the family's main breadwinner, financing the entire extended family. Her husband, Lito's *lolo*, was a quiet and passive man who kept mostly to himself. He was a lawyer by profession.

During the first session, the mother and father came with Lito. I was able to see Lito in two other sessions. But after these two sessions, the *lola* called up to cancel the next appointment because there was "no car available." In another instance, she asked to move the appointment to a later hour, as she had an emergency operation. I did not accommodate her request to postpone the appointment, since I had a series of appointments scheduled every hour of that day. Lito felt very bad about this, so I explored the possibility of his taking a cab or riding a bus. However, there was more to the problem than just transportation difficulty. I told him to bring his *lola* because I wanted to talk to her. I did not want to see him on and off when it was obvious the *lola* called the shots. Hence, I waited for him to bring along his *lola* and left the door open, so to speak.

He did not come for two weeks until, one day the *lola* called for an urgent appointment. I scheduled her as I would schedule any other client. She came without a fuss, and brought a letter Lito had written and which she found in a drawer. In the letter, Lito had said that were he not allowed to see me, he could not get well, since I was the only person in the world who really understood him. This jolted the *lola*, who has cooperated very well since then. The *lola* was genuinely concerned about Lito, but she could not get herself to accept that her grandson had to see a psychologist at the start of the therapy.

It was obvious from this case that if I, as a therapist, failed to include the *lola* — who was the power and decision-maker — I would have missed the boat. It was of utter significance to make the *lola* understand Lito's situation, so that she could even become the therapeutic ally in the family later. Had the *lola* not been convinced that Lito's therapy sessions were important, a power play could have ensued between the *lola* and me, and she would have continued to sabotage the therapy.

The therapy, however, did not foster dependency on the part of the IP. Because Lito was supported in the therapy and no more sabotage took place, he was able to go back to school. In fact, he took his studies seriously, and even got a part-time job because he wanted to support himself through college.

The Lola Who Is Ill

René was an eight-year-old boy who was brought in for therapy by his parents for he would cry excessively, scream, be unable to sleep, and utter such depressive statements like "I wish I could just die so no one will have any more problems in the family."

From the initial interview, I gathered that René lived with his paternal grandmother on weekdays, and would be fetched by his parents on Saturday afternoons. He would then be brought back to his *lola* on Sundays at five o'clock in the afternoon.

His parents got alarmed because René would scream and cry every time they would take him home with them. When he was with them, he would talk about how *kawawa* (pitiful) his *lola* was and would call her up on the phone. He also became very agitated and nervous as 5 p.m. drew near, since this meant going back to his *lola*. He had a hard time sleeping at night because he was afraid his *lola* would get sick. It turned out that every time his parents were late in bringing him back (at exactly 5 p.m.), the *lola* would get very ill.

The whole thing started when René was "lent" to the *lola* — a common enough practice in large Filipino families. One child is made to live with the *lola*, who needs someone to keep her company. Sometimes, it can happen that the parents are unable to support or to send one of their children to school. They then "lend" the child to the *lola*. This is done for the aging *lola*, who needs someone to provide her with the gaiety and joy that only a child can give.

In René's case, everything came about not because his parents could not afford to support him, for they were earning enough for their small family. It all began as a casual practice of leaving René with his *lola* on Sundays, when they had their customary family lunches together. The *lola* would later ask René to stay on till Monday, at times till Tuesday, and so on. Furthermore, the *lola* would give him a lot of toys and other things he wanted.

Before they realized it, René was staying with his *lola* more often than with his own parents. He would go home to them only during weekends. When René turned six and was ready for formal schooling, his parents decided to get him back, so they could supervise his schooling properly. But the *lola* became ill and had to be hospitalized at the time they wanted to get René back. They had to wait for her to recover. Doctors diagnosed her to be hypersensitive, with a heart ailment. Since her blood pressure could easily shoot up, it was imperative to keep her calm and controlled.

René's parents made subsequent attempts to get him back, but each time the *lola* became unfailingly ill. They had to keep delaying until, finally, René's mother put her foot down. She could no longer bear René's crying, sad demeanor, nervousness, and inability to sleep while with them. Even René's only sibling, a younger sister, became upset and wondered why her brother did not live with them. The husband tried to talk about the problem with his mother (the *lola*), but each time he did so, her blood pressure would rise. This emotional "blackmailing" went on for several months and caused marital problems for René's parents. Arguments and quarrels became more frequent between them. The mother felt that her husband should be able to assert himself vis-à-vis his mother. Although he fully understood his wife, the husband could not risk causing his mother's illness, lest he be blamed for an ensuing death. What made the parents finally decide to seek help was René's worsening condition. He became very nervous, restless, and at one point, even screamed at his parents, "I don't love you! I hate you! I hate you!" This caused extreme anxiety in his parents, especially in the mother who felt even more helpless.

Being the daughter-in-law, she could not deal directly with the *lola*. The mother needed her husband's support, at the same time feeling it was high time that her husband put his foot down. The husband was in a very difficult position, as he was caught between his wife and his mother. Besides, the illness of the *lola* was real. He would not be able to forgive himself should anything happen to his mother because of him. After a few sessions threshing out the complications of the situation, they were ready to discuss the possible solutions.

It was now clear that the main source of René's stress was his conflict in trying to please both his *lola* and his parents. He was ridden with guilt for his sick *lola*. The image of his *lola* lying down in bed, breathing painfully, remained vivid in his mind even after he had left her home. On the other hand, he wanted to be with his sister very much, but was utterly confused about his feelings toward his parents. Why could they not solve the problem for him? Why were they causing his *lola*, who was so good to him, to suffer so much? He knew he rightly belonged to his parents and sister, and this made him feel guilty too.

In discussing the alternatives, one main consideration was to minimize immediately the tension arising from René's feeling of being torn between his *lola* and parents. If the adults could agree on a way of not further dividing his loyalties, his anxiety and nervousness would immediately decrease. The possibility of talking to the *lola* was explored, but this proved to be a dead end. Nobody could touch the *lola* because all those concerned were afraid to cause illness and possible death. Nobody could afford to have that kind of guilt on his or her conscience. The *lola* would not agree to talk to a professional either.

Facing that dead end, the parents decided not to make a fuss about Rene's living with his *lola*. They would thus lessen the conflict by removing one source of pressure for René — the pressure coming from them. If only to reduce the conflict for Rene, they were willing to let the *lola* win.

With the power in the hands of the sick *lola*, there seemed to be no better alternative. The "tyranny of the weak" was how the mother aptly termed it. The arrangement was explained to René who seemed to understand. He was assured of his parents' love in order that he would not take their decision as a sign of rejection or of giving up.

The Financier-Aunt

The financier-aunt usually has a good-paying job, and still lives with her parents if they are alive. She takes care of them financially, at least in part. She is usually unmarried, strict, and has a lot of money. She is the one looked up to and relied on to make decisions. Her opinion is always sought by her mother.

Ester was a graduate student in psychology while also enrolled in medicine — two very demanding courses. She lived with her aunt while her parents were in the United States. Her heart was in psychology, but the aunt who had financed her schooling since she was in grade school wanted her to take up medicine. Ester tried to explain her side, but her aunt would not hear any of her reasons. The aunt took a very firm stand on this matter.

Ester was almost through with her graduate studies in psychology, but was just starting out in her medical course. Once, in the middle of the semester, she almost broke down in exhaustion. During her consultation with me, she expressed how angry she was about having to take up medicine. She felt helpless and powerless about the situation, however. She felt it would be foolish to give up her graduate studies, for she really loved psychology. Besides, it was now almost completed.

Long-distance conversations with her parents did not prove useful, since they insisted that she obey her aunt, who happened to be older than her mother. The aunt was the *ate* whose decisions were always followed in the family. After all possible alternatives were explored, Ester ended up having to cope with both courses and released her frustration and tension on her friends. She was dependent on her aunt for survival, therefore, she could not be ungrateful or *walang utang na loób*.

Another case dealing with the financier-aunt's power was that of Edgar, who was brought in to see me by his mother for refusing to go to school and for certain changes in his behavior. He was quite sociable, yet now had become shy and nervous.

About six months before the referral, Edgar's father left for Saudi Arabia to augment the family's finances. The mother has difficulty adjusting to her new life situation, for she used to be so dependent on her husband.

After talking to Edgar and his mother, it became clear to me that the mother depended a lot on her elder sister (the aunt and also the IP's godmother) for any important decision. The aunt was also financing the therapy sessions, and she wanted a talk with me.

I found out from my session with her that she was in charge of Edgar's schooling and was paying for his tuition. The aunt further explained that the mother did not really understand her son, and even insisted that Edgar was merely *nakulam* or *pinasukan ng demonyo* (possessed by the devil) which the aunt herself did not believe in. The mother and aunt did not agree on what was wrong with Edgar, though the mother, being subservient to her *ate*, did not openly assert herself. Their disagreements, although not exhibited openly, troubled and confused Edgar and made him more nervous and insecure. He felt he should obey his aunt but also pitied his mother who seemed weak and lost. Edgar became more inactive and "paralyzed" as if his body was preventing him from moving. In fact, his drawings were very rigid and he used a ruler all the time. It was also difficult for him to express himself verbally and say things about himself.

The therapy would not be effective if the mother and the aunt did not see eye to eye, so I had a session with both of them to explain the dynamics of Edgar's behavior in the light of family events, primarily his father's departure for Saudi Arabia.

The Authoritative Patriarch

In my experience, given our matriarchal society, it seems more difficult to find the authoritative patriarch than the dominating matriarch. Because the case presented in detail in the preceding chapter clearly portrays the dominating matriarch, I shall not include in the present chapter a separate case description of this more commonly encountered pattern.

The authoritative patriarch is usually the father who is the sole breadwinner of the family, while the mother is usually the younger and less accomplished one. She probably has not experienced holding a job or if she has one, it is usually low-paying and she automatically gives this up after marriage or the birth of the first child. The father usually demands of his wife good care of the household and the children: The house must run smoothly and the children must all be healthy and well-behaved.

Cynthia, an eight-year-old girl, was the second in a family of three children. She was referred to me by her mother for her irritating behavior, namely, forgetting to brush her teeth at night and moving too slowly in the morning, making her sister nervous about being late for school. The elder sister, on the other hand, was a good girl who did everything right. She was, however, very compulsive and uptight — a perfectionist, in short.

The family would move to different locations, depending on the demands of the father's job. When the father needed to be out of the country for a long time, the whole family had to go along. Wherever they lived, the same expectations of proper behavior were required of the children.

When Cynthia began to act out, the mother discussed it with her husband. However, he would not really listen to her, brushing the problem off as a very minor thing that the mother should be able to handle herself. The mother in turn began to feel more and more inadequate because the harder she tried, the more stubborn and willful Cynthia became. Furthermore, because she was financially dependent on her husband, she could only casually mention to him wanting to seek professional help for Cynthia. The idea was unacceptable to him. The mother naturally resented this negative attitude. She felt that only his job and making a lot of money mattered to him, as he did not take part in the household or family problems. She decided to seek help secretly. She gained insights regarding her compulsive need to prove herself that she was a good wife and mother. Previously, she had felt she failed as a mother when her daughter acted out or rebelled against her.

Owing to her husband's demands on her, she in turn became extremely demanding of herself and her two daughters.

In effect, the *ate* reacted by being a perfectionist, while the second girl asserted herself by disobeying her mother. Yet, even after the mother gained insight and took concrete coping steps (such as providing behavioral charts for good behavior, allowing the children to have more free and play time, and to go out with their respective friends), she became increasingly depressed upon realizing that her husband did not really understand her. He even made her feel more incompetent for not being able to handle "such simple things."

It was not until she finally got sick with mild heart palpitations that the husband got worried for the first time. Upon her discharge from the hospital, he agreed to accompany her for therapy sessions. It took only two sessions for their problems to be resolved. The mother took a part-time job, which made her feel good about herself. She did not even have to be so perfectionistic and demanding of her children anymore, because she now had another source for her self-esteem and feeling of competence. Consequently, too, when the husband became more aware of his wife's need, he learned to listen and became more emotionally involved with the family. Even better, he became less rigid and he realized he was benefiting from his wife's opinion and suggestions regarding his business concerns.

Another example was that of Gabby, a ten-year-old boy who was restless, inattentive, and effeminate. His father was a very accomplished economist while his mother was a housewife. He had a younger sister. At the time of the referral, his mother felt anxious and defeated because she did not know how to handle her son's behavior. The mother was a sensitive and emotional person, while the father was so rigid and authoritative that nobody dared to ask him questions. Whatever he ordered was immediately done.

The dynamics of this family are similar to those operating in the previous case. The drawing of Gabby (figure 28) eloquently speaks for itself; it gives us a very good picture of the family dynamics in terms of who holds the power. In the drawing, the father is lording it over the whole family. Gabby drew himself as almost drowning under his authority. On the other hand, his mother, and the youngest brother — who was

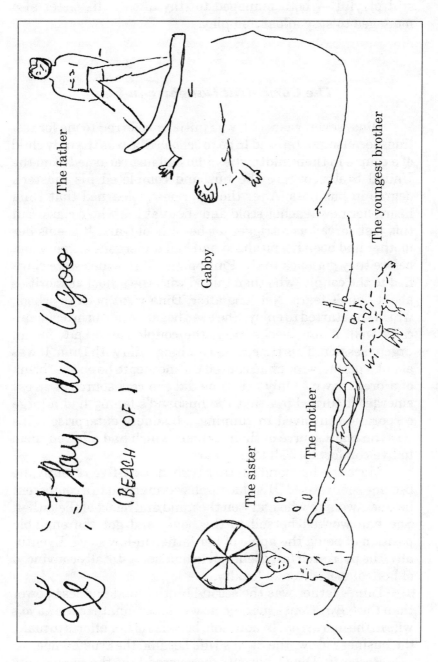

Figure 28. Gabby's Drawing: "The Power in My Family"

still playful — both managed to stay afloat. His sister also managed to stay afloat and play.

The Competent Daughter-in-Law

Dina, seven years old, was initially referred to me for testing, because she refused to go to school. She was the only child of a couple in their midthirties who had just returned from the United States, where the husband completed his master's degree in business. After the interview, I learned that Dina heard her new teacher scold and shout at the whole class. But this just served as a trigger for her school fears. It seems her mother had been hospitalized and had undergone surgery just before they got back to the Philippines. The issues were clarified to the couple, who then talked with the school authorities about Dina's fears. Not long after, Dina went back to school, which she started to enjoy. She even began to perform academically well. A few weeks later, the couple came back for an urgent session. This time, it had nothing to do with Dina. It was about a problem that had caused the mother to be on the "brink of a breakdown." Only this time did the real source of stress emerge. It turned out that the husband's family had a large corporation involved in running a business enterprise. This was the main source of their income, which had allowed them to live comfortably all these years.

Since the husband's father turned sixty-five recently, he became semiretired. His eldest son was married to a competent businesswoman who had won the mind and heart of the father. She had worked herself to the bone, and got the enviable position of being the apple of her father-in-law's eye. Eventually, the patriarch fully believed in her, being totally convinced of her competence and loyalty.

Dina's father was the second brother and had less power than the *kuya*. Consequently, he was subordinate to the *kuya*'s wife in the hierarchy. In addition, because of her efforts to make the business grow, the *kuya*'s wife became the trusted one.

Recently, Dina's parents discovered that the *kuya*'s wife had manipulated the situation further, becoming the next biggest stockholder in the company, aside from being the vice-president — a position created by the old man. Moreover, she bought several choice lots to her name and, to make matters worse, she started to treat her brother-in-law and his wife rudely. The *kuya*'s wife was practically running the corporation — a situation which the *kuya* seemed to enjoy too. At times, she would even very subtly give out statements about her hold on her father-in-law, the patriarch.

The couple tried to bring up this issue with the father, who refused to listen, as he could not believe anything negative about the *kuya*'s wife. Getting no positive results, they talked the problem over with the mother (the patriarch's wife). She could not do much, however. She did not know anything about the business, for she was a full-time housewife.

Desperate and angry, Dina's parents came to me for help to clarify their options and plan what they wanted with their lives. Because their marriage was solid, it was easy for them to decide to leave the country instead of getting caught in a poisonous web, which created so much strong feelings of help-lessness and heaviness in both of them. Because they genuinely cared for each other, they strengthened their togetherness by clarifying their frustrations to each other, as well as the source of strength between the two of them and their only child, Dina. Despite this, they still had a hard time letting go of the family business, because they felt the patriarch was being deceived. However, they had done their best and it was the patriarch who refused to listen to them. They could not waste their lives trying to convince him.

There are different variations of this configuration, like the competent son-in-law or nephew. The dynamics are similar and clearly identifiable.

The Child Tyrant

Mark, eight years old, was in the clinic of a pediatrician, where he had been waiting with his mother and many other parents for their turn. When I came to him, I saw him shouting at his mother (in Filipino): "You're ugly, I hate you! I'm going to kick you!" And he actually kicked his mother. This left the poor mother helpless and extremely embarrassed.

As expected, Mark also tried to take me on. Noticing that I was not budging from the firm and consistent limit I had set with him, he settled down and listened to me. His testing the limits was over, at least with me.

Upon talking with the mother, I found out that the father, who was out of the house most of the time, believed that Mark would eventually outgrow his stubbornness. She also revealed they lived with the *lola* (maternal grandmother) who interfered every time she tried to discipline Mark. Mark had a mild neurological problem and had some seizures occasionally. But these seizures were almost completely under control when a pediatric neurologist prescribed medication and monitored his reactions. Previous to this, Mark would have an attack every time he got scolded. This scared the mother and the *lola*, who gave in to all of Mark's wishes and desires.

Because the seizures had been taking place since he was five years old, Mark eventually got used to getting his own way. He sensed he had control over everyone in the family, even if he was troublesome. Underneath the "powerful" tyrant was actually a very negative self-concept. He knew he was a bad boy, and the knowledge did not make him feel good about himself. He was also very ambivalent about the authority figures in his life. He was angry with his parents, as well as with his *lola*, for not setting limits on him. In other words, he was angry at them for allowing him to become a bad boy.

A spoiled child or a child tyrant often holds a position of power, but underneath that power-trip, the child actually feels a rejection. He or she senses that the adults who are supposed to set limits are giving up on him or her. As in an impulse-control problem, the child cannot yet set the limits for himself. Hence, an anarchy of impulses takes place, which the child is left to deal with all by himself. The child sees authority figures, when not firm enough, as helpless. And should this happen, the power becomes frightening, overwhelming, and "bad" to the child's mind.

The All-Knowing Yaya

The *yaya* (child caretaker) seems to have become a permanent fixture in Filipino homes. Among families from the lower middle to the upper socioeconomic levels, there is almost always a *yaya* as long as there are young children. The mother is dependent on the *yaya* for the care of her young offspring, especially if she is a working mother and the older siblings are in school. Sometimes, the mother is not aware of what the *yaya* does with the child, because other people in the household are afraid to tell on her. There have been cases of the *yaya* locking a child up in the closet or bathroom for hours, resulting in the child's mutism or speech delay. Some *yaya* have also been known to force-feed children under their care, resulting in a trauma for eating — as happened in the following case.

Alfonso, three and a half years old, was brought in to see me for what his parents termed a "feeding problem." It turned out that, for about a year now, Alfonso was not taking anything but milk, which had to be spoonfed to him. Before he turned two and shortly after, Alfonso was eating "fast and plenty." But when he was about two and a half, he was observed to scream hysterically at feeding time. He would hardly open his mouth to swallow the milk. If the milk had not been forced on him, he would probably need to be fed intravenously. Alfonso was also observed to be fearful of new places and people.

The parents were both running their own business, on which they had to concentrate, else the business would fold up. Alfonso was therefore largely left to the care of his *yaya*. There was no known trauma associated with their child's developmental milestones. Pregnancy and delivery were normal. Apgar score at birth was ten. Speech and motor development were normal, and even slightly advanced. The only possible source of trauma was the father's leaving for the United States on Alfonso's birthday, and his coming back after six months only to leave again for a year. Only later did the mother discover through another maid that Alfonso's *yaya* had been force-feeding him. If he refused to eat, she would heat the food until it was piping hot, then force him to eat it. If he resisted, she would recline his body and stick the spoon with hot food into his mouth.

The mother had wondered why the *yaya* would close the door and turn on the TV while feeding Alfonso. Because she was afraid to lose the services of the *yaya*, however, she did not investigate any further. The *yaya*, feeling she was indispensable, felt her power even more, she even threatened the other maids if they told on her. A lot of times, she would also tell the mother how to do things since she was the experienced one.

Rudy, seven years old, was another victim of the *yaya*'s power. Though the mother sensed that the *yaya* was too stern and hard on him, she rationalized this by saying he needed to be disciplined. It turned out that, although the *yaya* would punish him, she also spoiled him and did everything for him, like dressing him up and bathing him. Rudy therefore became very attached to her. The mother was a very busy business-woman who could not afford to lose the *yaya*'s services. The *yaya* had become so powerful she would even close the door of Rudy's room and not allow the mother to come in — on the pretext of disciplining him. Sensing her power, the *yaya* even extended her rules to the entire household. Only when Rudy turned seven did the mother come to her senses. She summoned enough courage to dismiss the powerful *yaya*.

Further Discussion

From the preceding examples, it becomes clear that before beginning to make changes in the family system, the therapist must decipher who wields the **power in the family**, so that treatment can be effected. More importantly, the therapist must not get caught in a power play.

The **power** patterns identified in this chapter are preliminary insights on the concept of power in the Filipino family. They point to an important consideration when deciphering the power in the family — that of looking at the extended family. We saw this in the cases of the dominant and sick lola and the financier aunt.

The cases also highlight the necessity of examining the **present living** unit, which may include nonfamily members, as in the case of the all-knowing *yaya*. Although the *yaya* is not an actual member of the nuclear family or of the extended family, she may be a very significant figure in the household.

As he looks into the dynamics of the total system, the reader might also be reminded of the need to consider the concept of **power** together with the three other previously mentioned dimensions of family functioning. Does the power-holder have a high or low ***degree of anxiety***? What ***capacity*** has he ***to change***? Does the ***symptom-carrier*** have the power as in the case of the child tyrant? An effective treatment plan is usually based on an analysis of the configuration of the four dimensions — in relation to the total system.

An understanding of this configuration helps the family therapist not to get caught in a power play and in sabotage games which could diminish his or her own power to heal.

Healthy families are usually able to maintain a flexible system where power is shared. Depending on the kind of stress, they are able to shift power from one member to another and not allow one member to hold on to the power rigidly.

A Postscript

THE TOPICS IN THIS BOOK have generated questions that are stimulating and compelling subjects for more systematic research. For example, who becomes the *IP*, or *Identified Patient,* in the Filipino family? Is it the *ate*, the *kuya*, the middle sibling, or the *bunso*? Is it necessarily the child who is different from the rest, as in the case of the autistic child?

Does physical appearance, together with the *family mythology*, play a significant role, as in the case of the child who looks like the "crazy" uncle or the famous *lolo*?

The factors mentioned are important, but there is reason to believe that it is the child — the most sensitive, most attuned, most caring, and most concerned about keeping the family intact and happy — who turns out to be the IP or the symptom-carrier. The child takes it upon himself or herself to act out and signal for help. A better knowledge of children's characteristics therefore could help parents become more alert in picking up these signals.

What specific coping strategies do children in the poor and rural areas employ when their families are under stress? They seem to have more direct ways of handling their situation, as was evident in the case of the eight-year-old girl who confronted her father's *querida* — in contrast to the indirect manner those on a higher socioeconomic stratum face the same problem.

A more thorough understanding of the family dynamics and of the systemic approach could be used in helping child prostitutes and other street children. For those among them who have no more families, perhaps "new" families could be constituted or foster families carefully selected. What are more concrete ways of forming, rebuilding, and strengthening Filipino marriages so that they can continue to be the pillars and architects of our families?

Stages of family development could be better studied starting with the young couple, to the couple with young children, to those with adolescent children, and so on, to the couple at the "empty nest" stage, who have come full circle, and have only each other to face once more. Is the "empty nest" stage a common phenomenon among Filipino families — or are we able to keep the tradition of grandparents living with and being surrounded by their grandchildren?

How can we encourage the *tagasaló* to keep the endearing trait of caring for others without becoming compulsive about it? What concrete childrearing practices can be introduced in order to balance the "taking care" behavior between men and women? What happens to a child caretaker like René when he grows up and has his own family? Why does he not seem to develop into the nurturing male that most marriages lack? It would be worthwhile to study and pinpoint the specific childrearing practices that nip in the bud the development of the caring Filipino male.

In the families of the not-so-special children and the compulsive *tagasaló*, what role does favoritism play? How does favoritism tie up with family mythologies? It would be interesting to explore further the myth that parents should and could feel the same way toward all their children. Since each child is unique, different feelings are evoked by each child. A parent may find it effortless to communicate with one child and extremely difficult to do so with another. What specific elements constitute this connection or "chemistry" in the interaction between parents and child? It would be helpful to study the phenomenon of favoritism in relation to the *tagasaló* and the *Identified Patient* and to look into the modes and patterns of communication within their family systems.

More in-depth studies could shed light on the coping mechanisms of the siblings of suicides.

Another suggestion for further research is the question of who becomes the power in the family. Contrary to popular expectations, age does not seem to be the determining factor, as in the case of the sick *lola* and the child tyrant. Is *the power* the one who can arouse sympathy or guilt in others?

Patterns of power and analysis of family dynamics could perhaps be applied to business establishments and government institutions. The research implications are many and intriguing when we consider the family as a microcosm of the larger society.

In this book, the different concepts in *family systems theory* were presented through case studies. As the cases became alive through this approach, the concepts have, it is hoped, been absorbed and learned "painlessly." At the same time, I hope that the basic principles of family therapy have come through as a running thread, uniting all the chapters in my emphasis on the family systems approach as the significant point of view in therapy. Each presented problem or chief complaint was viewed and situated in the context of the family and extended family. This once more underscored the importance of the interrelationships among family members as they all try to live in harmony and equilibrium.

The cases were not exhaustive, and their choice was determined mainly by what stood out in my experience.

Many more problems in the family have not been included in this book, but I hope that this presentation represents only the beginning of an effort among professionals and parents to explore more creative ways of keeping the Filipino family intact and fully functional.

In this way, we can all help the Filipino family to continue being the solid ground on which to stand as we face the stresses in rebuilding this nation.

Appendix

Form Filled Out by Examiner
(Adapted from French 1977)

I. IDENTIFYING DATA

Names of

Identified Patient _____

Mother _____

Father _____

Others in living unit _____

Address:_____

Phone: home _____

work _____

National Origin _____

Socioeconomic Level: (1-5) (1 = highest, 5 = lowest)

Identified Patient _____

Age _____ years and _____ months

Date of birth _____

Ordinal position _____ of _____

School

    Name _____
    Phone _____
    Teacher _____
    Grade _____
    (Special placement?) _____

Referral Source

    Name _____
    Phone _____

Previous Therapists

    Name _____
    Phone _____
    Seen from _____ to _____

II. CLINICAL PROBLEM

A. Chief complaints:

    Identified Patient _____
    Parents _____
    School _____
    Others _____

B. Duration and progression of the problem:

C. Major life changes:

D. Special problems (legal, medical, etc.):

III. TEMPERAMENTAL TYPE
As Described by Parents

Trait	Infancy	Childhood	Currently Observed
Activity level	____	____	_____
Adaptability	____	____	_____
Rhythmicity	____	____	_____
Mood	____	____	_____
Approach/ withdrawal	____	____	_____
Intensity of reaction	____	____	_____
Threshold	____	____	_____
Persistence/ attention span	____	____	_____
Distractibility	____	____	_____

IV. CHILD'S DEVELOPMENTAL HISTORY

Stage	Biological	Psychological	Family	Social
Prenatal (parental expectations)	____	____	____	____
Pregnancy and delivery	____	____	____	____
A. Infancy (basic trust vs. mistrust)	____	____	____	____
B. Toddlerhood (autonomy vs. shame and doubt)	____	____	____	____
C. Preschool (initiative vs. guilt)	____	____	____	____
D. Grade school (industry vs. inferiority)	____	____	____	____

V. FAMILY TREE

VI. FAMILY'S LEVEL OF DIFFERENTIATION (1-5)

VII. PARAMETERS OF FAMILY FUNCTION

	Low	*High*
A. Anxiety	_____	_____
B. Capacity to change	_____	_____
C. Symptom-carrier role	_____	_____
D. Power	_____	_____

VIII. SUMMARY OF FAMILY DYNAMICS

IX. FORMULATION AND DIFFERENTIAL DIAGNOSIS

Biological factors:_____

Developmental factors:_____

Diagnosis:_____ Supporting data:_____

Current situational factors:_____

Current coping maneuvers:_____

Differential diagnosis (GAP Report No. 62): _____

X. PROBLEM-PLAN LIST

Level	*Problem*	*Plan*
Biological	_____	_____
Psychological	_____	_____
Family	_____	_____
Social	_____	_____

References Cited

Adams, M. 1971. *Mental Retardation and Its Social Dimensions*. New York: Columbia University Press.

Andolfi, M. 1979. *Family Therapy: An Interactional Approach*. New York: Plenum Press.

Bandler, R. 1985. *Using Your Brain —for a Change*. Utah: Real People Press.

Bowen, M. 1976. Theory in the Practice of Psychotherapy. In Guerin (ed.) *Family Therapy: Theory and Practice*. New York: Gardner Press.

Bowen, M. 1978. *Family Therapy in Clinical Practice*. New York: Jason Aronson.

Bulatao, J., S.J. 1981. *Essays and Studies*. Rosalinda Castiglioni (ed.) Quezon City: Ateneo de Manila Press.

Carandang, M.L.A. 1979. The Filipino Child in the Family: A Developmental Approach. *Philippine Studies* 27:469-82.

_____. 1981. The Rubik's Cube Approach: A Multidimensional Model for Working with Children. *Philippine Journal of Psychology* 14 (1 & 2):47-54.

_____. 1984. The Dynamics of Stress and Coping

Among Filipino Families in the Context of the Present Socio-Political Crisis. Paper presented at the Psychological Association of the Philippines' Twentieth Annual Convention.

_____. 1985. The Practitioner as Researcher. Paper presented at the Psychological Association of the Philippines' Twenty-first Annual Convention.

Erikson, E. 1963. *Childhood and Society*. New York: W.N. Norton.

French, A.P. 1977. *Disturbed Children and Their Families*. New York: Human Sciences Press.

Guthrie, G. 1961. *The Filipino Child and Philippine Society: Research, Reports and Essays*. Manila: Philippine Normal College Press.

Jurilla, L. 1986. An Exploratory Study of the Motivational System for Parenthood of Rural Married Couples. *Philippine Journal of Psychology* 19:5-17.

Laing, R.D. 1969. *The Politics of the Family and Other Essays*. New York: Random House.

Lapuz, L.V. 1977. *Filipino Marriages in Crisis*. Quezon City: New Day Publishers.

Minuchin, S. et al. 1967. *Families of the Slums: Exploration of Their Structure and Treatment*. New York: Basic Books.

Minuchin, S. 1974. *Families and Family Therapy*. Cambridge, Mass.: Harvard University Press.

Naval, T. 1979. Coping and Motivational Patterns of Children in Poverty Areas. *Philippine Studies* 27:505-26.

Rapaport, J. and Ismond, D. 1984. *DSM-III Training Guide for the Diagnosis of Childhood Disorders*. New York: Brunner/Mazel.

Satir, V.M. 1967. *Conjoint Family Therapy*. California: Science and Behavior Books.